Enhancing Culturally Inte
Safety Response in Musli

G000164812

This informative new volume presents the Culturally Integrative Family Safety Response (CIFSR) model that is currently being used by the Muslim Resource Centre for Social Support and Integration (MRCSSI) in London, Ontario. Created to support immigrant and newcomer families from collectivist backgrounds struggling with issues related to pre-migration trauma, family violence, and child protection concerns, the CIFSR model focuses on early risk identification and intervention, preserving safety, and appropriate conflict responses. Also included is a Q&A chapter from the authors that invites helping professionals, educators, and other readers to apply the model globally.

Mohammed Baobaid, PhD, earned his doctoral degree from the Institute of Psychology at the University of Erlangen Nurnberg in Germany and is currently the executive director and founder of the Muslim Resource Centre for Social Support and Integration (MRCSSI) in Canada. Dr. Baobaid has been instrumental in initiating research elements in works related to violence prevention including family violence and youth violence. For 30 years he has conducted research to identify the challenges of working with victims of family violence and youth violence in Yemen and Canada. His research resulted in developing culturally integrative family violence prevention and intervention strategies.

Lynda M. Ashbourne, PhD, RMFT, is an associate professor, family therapist, clinical supervisor, and instructor of novice couple and family therapists in the Department of Family Relations & Applied Nutrition at the University of Guelph in Ontario, Canada. Her research has focused on family relationships and the challenges to those of broader social influences such as migration. She has collaborated with Dr. Mohammed Baobaid since 2001 in considering how systemic and relational therapy practices can enhance work with families who have experienced global migration and pre- and post-migration influences of violence.

Enhancing Culturally Integrative Family Safety Response in Muslim Communities

Mohammed Baobaid and
Lynda M. Ashbourne

Routledge
Taylor & Francis Group

NEW YORK AND LONDON

First published 2017
by Routledge
711 Third Avenue, New York, NY 10017

and by Routledge
2 Park Square, Milton Park, Abingdon, Oxon OX14 4RN

*Routledge is an imprint of the Taylor & Francis Group, an informa
business*

British Library Cataloguing in Publication Data
A catalogue record for this book is available from the British Library

Library of Congress Cataloging in Publication Data
Names: Baobaid, Mohammed, author. | Ashbourne, Lynda M., author.
Title: Enhancing culturally integrative family safety response in Muslim
communities / Mohammed Baobaid and Lynda M. Ashbourne.
Description: New York, NY : Routledge, 2016.
Includes bibliographical references and index.
Identifiers: LCCN 2016019562 | ISBN 9781138948730 (hbk. : alk. paper) |
ISBN 9781138948747 (pbk. : alk. paper) | ISBN 9781315669489 (ebk)
Subjects: LCSH: Immigrant families--Services for--Canada. | Muslim
families--Services for--Canada. | Family services--Canada. | Family social
work--Canada. | Social work with immigrants--Canada. | Social work
with minorities--Canada.
Classification: LCC HV4013.C2 B36 2016 DDC 362.89/
9120882970971--dc23
LC record available at https://lccn.loc.gov/2016019562

ISBN: 978-1-138-94873-0 (hbk)
ISBN: 978-1-138-94874-7 (pbk)
ISBN: 978-1-315-66948-9 (ebk)

Typeset in Sabon
by Taylor & Francis Books

To our families, who have shared laughter and tears with us along our life journey,

To our colleagues and communities, who encourage and challenge us,

To the refugee families who have trusted us with their stories,

And to the students and you, the reader, who will take these ideas in new and exciting directions.

Mohammed and Lynda

Contents

Figures

Acknowledgements

This book represents the collective contributions of many persons who nurtured the seeds of an idea; put CIFSR into practice; listened, adapted, and redeveloped practices that work for family members, the broader community, and service-providing systems; and took part in ongoing discussions with researchers, service providers, and community members about what works and what doesn't. These people are too numerous to identify by name, but they have each contributed to making the current model what it is. In particular, we want to acknowledge the continued contributions of Eugene Tremblay, Hassna Nassir, Nada Nessan, Aruba Mahmud, Abir al Jamal, Yasmin Hussain, Tosha Densky, and Mavis Lau – without these caring and competent professionals, this book and model would not be in their current form. We also want to thank former and current families with whom we have worked and who have provided important feedback to us along the way. Our students have asked excellent questions and contributed to our thinking in a number of areas related to this model. The professionals and service providers at a wide range of service organizations with whom we've collaborated have also contributed their ideas to making the model more complete. And finally, we wish to thank our funders, in particular Ontario Trillium Foundation, Ontario Ministry of the Attorney General, London Community Foundation, Status of Women Canada, and Department of Justice Canada, who continue to believe in the value of putting these ideas into practice. We also appreciate the support provided by the University of Guelph.

1 Introduction

We are writing this book in order to share our ideas about how best to work together with members of collectivist communities to reduce family violence. This does not mean that we think noncollectivist or more individualist communities don't experience family violence. We do believe, however, that many of the interventions now used by North American institutions such as child protection agencies, legal and social service systems, and healthcare services have been developed within a more prominently individualist context and may not fit so well when working with collectivist communities. By collectivist, we refer to primary allegiance to a group (which may be defined by family ties, ethnic or national roots, tribe or caste). Of course the degree of collectivist or individualist orientation can vary across communities, and these are not discrete perspectives. Members of collectivist communities perceive that an overall benefit to the collective supersedes or at least equals that of individual benefit.

Introductory Note from Mohammed Baobaid

For most of my life, I have felt called to the issue of violence prevention, family violence in particular. Beginning in my homeland of Yemen in 1985, and following my training as a psychologist in Germany, I have developed a framework to better understand the complexity of youth and family violence within a collectivist cultural context. This has grown directly from my experience as a psychologist, community developer, and researcher in Yemen where I worked with families, children, and youth involved with the criminal justice system as well as time spent researching family violence. Since coming to Canada in 2000, I have continued working as a men's counsellor, family therapist, and researcher. I have been working in Canada to build bridges across diverse Muslim and more dominant cultures, contributing to greater mutual understanding and social inclusion while at the same time increasing safety and respect for victims of family violence in Muslim families. In my own thinking, I've appreciated opportunities to bring together ideas about a universal human experience and specific cultural contexts, as well as bringing peoples of individualist and collectivist worldviews into a shared dialogue with each other.

I have also appreciated the opportunity to provide leadership and work together with the staff of the Muslim Resource Centre for Social Support and Integration (MRCSSI) in London, Ontario, to develop effective responses to the complex needs of families with collectivist cultural backgrounds who are experiencing family violence. In partnership with community leaders throughout Canada, I have piloted cross-sectoral and cultural sensitivity training workshops that are designed to facilitate dialogue and collaborative learning about the issue of family violence and differences in cultural attitudes. These are important building blocks that can support social inclusion for dominant and nondominant ethnic communities across Canada and beyond. Our recent work with child protection agencies in Ontario has contributed to a significant reduction in the number of Muslim children in care and in innovative practices and partnerships across several diverse communities.

Working collaboratively with Lynda Ashbourne for over a decade has been a great opportunity to bring together our ideas in a way that has enhanced the development of our model of intervention within a collectivist cultural context. Bringing different perspectives to the work in which we have been involved jointly has enriched our knowledge and has led us to put together this book. This book is important to me as a means of communicating with professionals, policy makers, and researchers about effective strategies for balancing safety concerns of victims of family violence while understanding and respecting their core values as members of collectivist communities.

Introductory Note from Lynda M. Ashbourne

I have been a family therapist, working systemically with individuals, couples, and families, for almost 25 years in a range of rural and urban communities with both settled and newcomer communities. I also teach and mentor new therapists who are learning to work with a broad range of clients, with specific attention to the broader system in which these clients live, work, and play. In particular, I attempt to instill an appreciation for the relationships and context in which people live (their family and close relationships; connections to broader family network and significant others; neighbourhood, migration, and newcomer status; cultural values and beliefs including religious and ethnic traditions; class, employment, and financial resources; illness, health, and trauma experience; availability and accessibility of broader system services and resources) and other aspects of people's day-to-day lives. I have learned a great deal from listening closely to how people describe what is important to them both in terms of how they perceive their problems and how they go about addressing them. I have appreciated working closely with Mohammed Baobaid for almost 15 years and learning so much from him about collectivist communities and their needs, particularly as new Canadians. I am not a newcomer, although my family history is full of migration stories. I have been privileged in many ways with respect to my social location. I have also learned from careful listening to the people who have consulted with me over the years about the troubles in their lives, often in the context of marginalization, transition, and social isolation. It is with great respect and appreciation for their wisdom and struggle that I bring forward their narratives in this work.

This book represents our attempt to capture our own learning and experience and that of MRCSSI in London, Ontario, Canada, as well as the voices of family members and service providers with whom we have spoken and worked over that same time period. We are writing primarily for service providers – those who work directly with individuals and families from collectivist communities – including child protection workers, social workers, family therapists, those who work in the court system, settlement workers, police personnel, and others. We hope that the ideas we present will encourage you to integrate a cultural perspective into your work, to consider how your formal training may have encouraged a more limited individualist focus that overlooks potential resources and particular needs of a collectivist community, and to engage and collaborate with cultural communities to prevent family violence and enhance family safety.

Muslim Resource Centre for Social Support and Integration

Founded in 2009 under the initiative of Mohammed Baobaid, MRCSSI is a not-for-profit organization with a goal of helping families and individuals overcome the challenges that impede their family safety. Recognizing that people coming from collectivist societies, like many Muslims in Canada, have unique challenges, MRCSSI seeks to support these families using a culturally integrative service. The history of MRCSSI dates back to 2003 with the establishment of the Muslim Family Safety Project based on research showing that local Muslim families who had been affected by family violence faced certain barriers in accessing and utilizing much needed services. This project was oriented around building bridges between local Muslim and Arab communities and established service providers in the broader community, and developing culturally appropriate responses to family violence. The importance of continued dialogue with existing agencies in order to reflect upon how to provide more accessible and culturally appropriate services has emerged as a fundamental element of the work of MRCSSI.

London is located in southwestern Ontario, Canada and is home to approximately 375,000 residents, of which approximately 25% are immigrants or refugees and approximately 10% are Muslim or Arabic speaking. Muslim refugees and immigrants come from a range of countries, including the United Kingdom, Lebanon, Somalia, Sudan, Yemen, Iraq, Pakistan, Bangladesh, Syria, Kurdistan, and Afghanistan, among others. According to Statistics Canada (2010), there are approximately 884,000 Muslims in Canada, constituting the largest religious minority nationally. London has a growing

Muslim population, the third largest in Canada. The Muslim population is not homogeneous; instead it is comprised of highly distinct and diverse groups, many of whom have emigrated from regions in Africa and Asia. Many recently arrived Muslim and Arabic immigrants in London have come from conflict zones and suffered intensive trauma.

Trauma, when not addressed, can be transmitted across generations and have a significant impact on family relationship patterns. These issues are compounded when other settlement stressors are present, for example, where there are few opportunities for employment due to language limitations or a lack of recognition of an immigrant's qualifications in Canada. Many recent arrivals are also single mothers either having lost the father of their children due to war or the father has been displaced by the war and accepted as a landed immigrant in a different country in Europe, Asia, or Oceania. These families are trying to reconstruct their lives. At times they are actively involved and preoccupied with the hopes of reuniting with the father or their adult children in danger back home. Extended family members, some of whom live nearby and some with whom they are still connected who live overseas, serve as their support. The stressors in their lives can compound and intersect to increase the risk of family conflict and violence.

Since 2009, MRCSSI programs, through partnership with established service-providing agencies in Ontario, have demonstrated success at reducing the escalation of violence, disruptions of families, and the number of children entering care. These programs have, most importantly, reduced the number of clients receiving court- and system-mandated services. At the same time, demand from within the Muslim and Arabic communities in London for these preventative services has increased significantly. The outcomes of de-escalating conflict and reducing episodes of family violence is due to the developing capacity of the community and partnered agencies to engage with MRCSSI collaboratively to seek solutions. With each successive implementation of programs by MRCSSI, the response goes deeper into engaging with the risk factors of violence while building community and service provider capacity to mobilize against family violence in a Culturally Integrative Family Safety Response (CIFSR). These are the ideas we write about here.

Culturally Integrative Family Safety Response

In Chapter 2, you will read about the CIFSR model in more detail. Simply put, this model places high priority on engaging all family members, including extended family, and coordinating supports around them that are oriented to the unique needs of the family. These supports are also extended to include collaboration between the service-providing agencies encircling the family and cultural organizations serving to maintain relationships and cultural awareness across these various systems. The goal is to increase safety and decrease the risk of violence. Where possible, the response entails early risk identification and intervention alongside an emphasis on utilizing the strengths and resources already present in the family and community. The model orients around preserving safety while also building community and family capacity for responding appropriately to family conflicts. We see this model as extending current efforts to provide translators, enhance cultural awareness in service agencies, and reach out to various communities to educate newcomers about their rights and available services. It takes into account the complex constellation of pre-migration trauma, the effects of migration and structural disruption on the family, and unique aspects of collectivist cultural and religious practices and social organization.

The balance of this book presents the experience of MRCSSI in piloting and adapting these ideas into practice. Where we can, we provide specific examples of responses in unique circumstances, including the feedback we have received from service providers about these responses. It is difficult to capture directly the voices of the family members with whom we have worked. Questions related to confidentiality and to the ethics of asking people to reflect on the resolution or ongoing presence of complex concerns in their lives have limited our ability to solicit and present these family member voices here. When we invite feedback about interventions, it is not surprising that comments are almost exclusively about the personal connections that family members have experienced with a particular therapist or counsellor. The broader systemic and multi-provider interventions that we see as being helpful to clients is happening at an organizational and community level that, while ultimately contributing to positive outcomes, is likely less visible or tangible at the interpersonal level. In providing case examples, we have attempted to present family members' experiences as closely as we can. We have protected their identity by removing identifying details and presenting case examples based on actual families and service-providing agencies in various communities in Ontario, Canada. In each chapter we have attempted to present challenges and opportunities, capacity and engagement of community and service-provider systems, and examples of work with families, as well as feedback from community service providers.

A note here about our use of various "voices" in our writing – you will find that the language we use is somewhat changeable over the course of the book. We have struggled a bit with this – recognizing that "we" can be used to obscure some important differences in context, and that a more formalized language can also obscure the personal, political, and contextualized nature of family and community lives and interactions. Where there is a particular section that presents the reflections of one of us, we have used "I" and indicated whether this refers to Mohammed or Lynda. Where individual practitioners, training participants, and service providers are quoted, we do not include actual names but designate clearly the position from which each person is reflecting on CIFSR practices. We trust that you will be patient with the inevitable gaps and overlaps, or the shifts in perspective that attend this multiplicity of voices, and hope that we have maintained clarity in presenting our understanding and experience.

The CIFSR model coordinates support around families and service agencies to increase safety and decrease risk on all levels of a violence and conflict continuum. This holistic approach reflects a corresponding continuum of responses that include prevention, early identification and early intervention, and critical intervention approaches. Chapter 3 presents prevention strategies directed at stopping family violence before it occurs. We describe prevention efforts at the level of communities and organizations, as well as with individual families.

Chapter 4 outlines the CIFSR model further along the response continuum where early identification and interventions allow a response to family situations before they escalate and require mandated service involvement (e.g., child protection). Here we also present in some detail the Four Aspects Screening Tool (FAST) and the Coordinated Organizational Response Team (CORT) developed as part of the CIFSR model.

Chapter 5 describes CIFSR in cases where the police, child protection, and/or other systems are already involved with families in collectivist communities in an attempt to address family violence and safety concerns. These critical interventions with more complex dimensions reflect family situations where there is high risk to family members' safety, and mandated service protocols that may make collaboration somewhat more challenging.

In Chapter 6 we present an analysis, primarily from Mohammed's perspective, of the CIFSR model in comparison with other culturally informed models of intervention with families.

Chapter 7 includes training implications associated with what we have learned from family members, service providers, and our own experience of putting these ideas into practice. This chapter is directed to those providing in-service and ongoing training for professionals who have been working in the field of family violence and child protection for a longer period of time, as well as those training new professionals. We also discuss in this chapter our ideas about providing support for community development that contributes to CIFSR-guided community practices.

Chapter 8, the final chapter, provides a dialogue between Mohammed and Lynda, describing what we believe we've learned and suggestions we have for future directions for service and research.

The Voices Informing this Book

This book represents the collective of persons who have contributed to the initial seeds of an idea; to putting CIFSR into practice; to listening, adapting, and coming back again to redeveloping a practice that works for family members, the broader community, and service-providing systems; and to ongoing discussions with researchers, service providers, and community members about what works and what doesn't. These people are perhaps too numerous to identify by name, but they have each contributed to making the current model what it is. In particular, we want to acknowledge the continued contributions of Eugene Tremblay, clinical director of MRCSSI. Eugene is a cofounder of the Safe Integration Program which led to the development of CORT and he has been the clinical lead for the CIFSR implementation. As well, the caring and competent professionals who have worked as integration counsellors and therapists at MRCSSI have put the ideas of CIFSR into their work with clients every day. We also want to acknowledge the voices of former and current families with whom we have worked, who have provided important feedback to us along the way. Our students have asked excellent questions and contributed to our thinking in a number of areas related to this model. The professionals and service providers at a wide range of service organizations with whom we've collaborated have also added their voices in making the model more complete.

This model and these practices are works in progress – they continue to evolve as we listen, observe, and adapt to the lived experiences of families and practitioners. We look forward to you, the reader, contributing your own voice to the ongoing development of theory and practice that leads to safer and more respectful family and community lives in diverse contexts.

2   The Culturally Integrative
Family Safety Response Model

The Culturally Integrative Family Safety Response (CIFSR) is a strengths-based response to family violence in collectivist immigrant families. Such a response engages all members of the family, including extended family and the broader collective. CIFSR coordinates highly individual supports around families and service agencies to increase safety and decrease risk of violence.

We refer to CIFSR practices as *culturally integrative responses to issues of family safety*. By this we mean that the model goes beyond "cultural sensitivity" (often addressed by educating service providers about cultural differences, providing language interpretation, and conducting outreach into under-serviced and diverse communities). In referring to "cultural integration," we mean that the model promotes dialogue between the minority collectivist community and the various agencies involved in anti-violence work in the broader community, while also integrating established best practices for serving families from more marginalized communities. In addition to the important aspects of service such as education, interpretation, and outreach, a *cultural broker* works with service providers to assist in the understanding of the unique aspects of each family's situation when they come into contact with the agency. As well, a broker organization can bring cultural communities and service agencies together to prepare coordinated prevention, awareness, and intervention materials and protocols.

The CIFSR model includes a *framework of family safety* that incorporates prevention and early intervention, even if this is somewhat outside of tradi-tional mandated services, and also attends to the resilience and strengths already present in the family and collective community. Over time, and regardless of the start or completion of interventions directed toward indi-vidual families, this practice model maintains attention to the concepts of *continuity of care* and *partnerships between established services and margin-alized cultural communities* as key to improving services provided to individuals and families more generally.

The CIFSR model promotes the importance of developing, strengthening, and sustaining relationships between service agencies and members of the cultural community – religious leaders, community leaders, and persons who represent the broader social fabric of a collectivist community – in a proactive manner. These relationships and ongoing interactions facilitate changing ideas and community norms around abuse and violence in families, as well as providing a more collaborative institutional response that is grounded in the local community and the broader system (police, court, child protection, professional services in the areas of counselling, etc.). The model promotes building relationships prior to specific interventions and recognizing the importance of these relationships over time. This allows for early intervention that includes measures of education, prevention, awareness, support, and collaboration with service providers, and encourages the development and provision of alternatives and supports that enhance safety and reduce risk for families. An example of CIFSR early intervention practices specifically linked to particular families and family members is the Safe Integration Project (SIP) offered by the Muslim Resource Centre for Social Support and Integration (MRCSSI). SIP organizes a collaborative community of service providers around a specific newcomer family in a pre-emptive move to support and assess potential for risk of violence when pre-migration trauma (often associated with migration from conflict zones) is an issue.

A note about terms – we are using the term "family violence" throughout this book as a broader term to include intimate partner violence, child abuse, and elder abuse within the context of family/intimate relationships. Family violence itself, as a concept and as understood by primarily Western societies, may be unfamiliar to many non-Western immigrants to Western countries who see what happens within families, including possible violence or aggression, as "private matters," and that others from outside the family do not have the right to intervene in these. An understanding of family violence will differ across cultures.

We also refer, from time to time, to "victims" and "perpetrators" of violence in families. We do so with the recognition that this is familiar language to service providers and professionals who work in the field of family violence and intimate partner violence. At the same time, as we will describe at various points, the line that marks an individual family member as solely a victim or solely a perpetrator of violence is not always clear. This is particularly the case when past intergenerational violence or trauma experiences related to war, political violence, or migration are inflicted on and influence some or all family members in diverse ways and to varying degrees. It may also be that the demarcation and/or terms themselves do not fit well with collectivist cultural understandings of conflict and violence in families or communities. We do not wish to oversimplify when we use these terms, and attempt to use them more as a means of describing application of service provider mandates.

In this book, we try to identify the potential gaps in services and responses to family violence in collectivist communities. We are particularly interested in what may be overlooked when identifying risk factors of family violence in the context of migration and culture, as well as protective factors that also reside within the family and/or the community of origin. We want to consider ways to move beyond improving the cultural sensitivity of established services and develop a different kind of response that integrates best practices of contemporary Western services with the cultural context of collectivist families. We see the CIFSR model as representing a way to engage in this type of response.

Theoretical Background

There are similarities in the starting points or underlying theories guiding CIFSR and other current directions in family-centred services. Practices such as family group conferencing, systems of care, and wraparound approaches are intentionally directed at honouring what the family knows, seeing positive potential and resourcefulness in families, and working in partnerships that are empowering and accountable to the people who are clients of these services (see Madsen, 2014, for a review of family-centred services). Laura Brown (2009) describes the importance of cultural competence that is integrated into good practice and points to the value of training that allows service providers to meet people where they are (seeing the unique aspects and intersections of culture and social location for each person) and practice self-awareness in terms of how their own social location influences what they see in others. Postmodern psychotherapy practices such as solution-focused and narrative interventions pay close attention to the individual strengths and resources of persons, as well as the stories we tell ourselves about how we got to be where we are currently and what is important to us.

The World Health Organization (WHO) (Krug, Dahlberg, Mercy, Zwi, & Lozano, 2002) identifies family violence as a public health issue internationally, taking an ecological stance that sees the problem as grounded in persons, relationships, community, and societal influences. Within this complex set of factors, WHO advocates for greater attention to cultural influences with respect to how family violence is experienced and addressed in various communities. In some parts of the world there is a decades-long history of developing and implementing strategies for addressing family violence – in others, this is a relatively new concern. Interventions tailored to diverse cultures or locations are, therefore, quite limited. Many of the interventions, practices, and policies that have been in place for longer periods of time are based on the values of more individualistic Western societies, where they have been developed. These approaches place the individual at the centre of interventions, and may disregard or pay scant attention to broader systemic and relational influences.

The CIFSR model we present here demonstrates one way of extending current ideas of resilience, family-centred care, cultural competence, and systemic influences beyond what has remained a fairly individualistic approach to working with an autonomous "self" or isolated nuclear family. We propose ways to augment current practices of putting the family first and attending to diversity by helping agencies and communities see how collectivist values and beliefs provide both untapped resources and overlooked challenges in working with families from collectivist communities.

Practice Orientation

CIFSR draws upon and extends current models of resilience- and solution-oriented practice in that it is oriented to not only building on the respective strengths of individuals, but also in identifying and building on the strengths and inherent resiliencies of collectivist communities. The model focuses on enhancing relationships between service providers and the collectivist community. This extends ecological models of community practice to a more explicit intention, when working with collectivist communities, to utilize the potential strengths of collectivism, address inherent challenges associated with beliefs and values held within these communities, and support the institutional structures around the community to act more collaboratively. This intentional awareness of collective and individual influences on members of minority collectivist groups in a predominantly individualist society enhances systemic and relational practices with individual families, family members, and the local community.

Collectivist Communities

Where individualist societies place a high value on autonomy and individuation from one's family of origin, collectivist societies place a greater emphasis on interdependence, obligation to the group, and social reputation. As much as 80% of the world population lives within authoritarian collectivist societies (Dwairy, 2002). Collectivist societies exist in many parts of the world, including Africa, the Middle East, Asia, South America, and the Pacific, as well as in minority communities that exist within broader individualist societies. Collectivism can refer to primary allegiance to the extended family, tribe, caste, ethnic group, or nation. Members of collectivist communities see that the overall benefit for the collective supersedes personal benefit, or at least carries equal weight. The entire family, and by extension, the collective community, is concerned about the reputation or standing of individuals given that the status of the family and collective is dependent on the behaviour of its members (Haj-Yahia & Sadan, 2008). Collectivist societies emphasize obedience and harmony, even in the face of personal cost for collaboration, in contrast to more individualistic and adversarial approaches (Yoishioka & Choi, 2005).

The ideal relationship between an individual's *self* and the collective has far-reaching implications for norms governing roles, responsibilities, and how one expresses oneself, as well as institutional practices and structures (Markus & Kitayama, 1994). Dwairy (2002) proposes that, in contrast to an internal psychological personality governing behaviour (as described within much of traditional Western psychology), those who live within a collectivist culture are influenced by their *social* and *private* layers of personality. The social layer, oriented to achieving reputation and honour while avoiding shame, ensures that most public behaviour is subject to authority, follows group rules, and is oriented to avoiding conflict. According to Dwairy, the private layer reflects those opinions or reactions that are not acceptable to the group, perhaps held back in public to avoid confrontation or shame, but which may be expressed when alone or with close family members. These behaviours may include violence or aggression, or what could be considered selfish or forbidden acts. Dwairy suggests that these two layers of collective personality act in tandem to influence behaviour, and that it is important to understand a person's level of individuation or interdependence as well as their cultural context and collective influences. Within the collective, social status, gender, and age determine who has authority and drives social interactions. Dwairy maintains that these factors are essential to understanding the behaviour of a person from a collectivist background, in contrast to considering internal psychological processes and temperament of a person from an individualist context.

While we have described the differences between individualist and collectivist societies in fairly stark terms here, we note that these aren't exclusive "groups." The example used most often for individualist culture is the US, and this is then extended to North America and Europe as Western cultures. At the same time, for example, there are major differences between the social policies of the US and Canadian universal health care or the social welfare systems of Northern Europe and Scandinavian countries. These latter types of policies might be considered to be more in tune with collectivist principles. For our purposes here, the Canadian context is important to note – in addition to some aspects of Canadian policy that may be a closer fit with collectivism, it is also the case that some more rural or isolated communities may function more collectively. It is an oversimplification to designate particular groups or persons as solely "collectivist" or "individualist." While we use these terms in this book to designate particular orientations, values, or organizing concepts that influence ideas about family, community, and the roles of service providers or intervention programs, we recognize that most people and communities fall somewhere on a continuum between these distinctions.

With specific regard to intimate partner violence directed toward women, we can see that a collectivist context could influence personal experience in some important ways. Haj-Yahia and Sadan (2008) provide some examples of this. They describe the ways that women in collectivist cultures who have experienced violence at the hands of their husbands may, for example, see damage or risk as directed not only toward themselves but also as threatening their extended family and collective. Similarly, Haj-Yahia and Sadan indicate that stereotypes identified within individualist cultures (such as blaming the woman for being in this situation or being a poor mother) can also be held in collectivist terms and will be further extended to her mother, sisters, and children. Further, in a context where submission and conflict avoidance are valued, and where preserving family relationships is paramount, women may feel forced to remain quiet about violence in their home at the risk of being seen as disruptive, rebellious, or disrespectful (Haj-Yahia & Sadan, 2008).

In such a context, women are most likely to approach close family members for support rather than more formal services, with respected members of the collective becoming involved if the situation escalates. These interventions and supports are likely to uphold the collectivist values of preserving the family and group norms, encouraging reconciliation, and potentially contributing to further feelings of powerlessness on the part of the woman. Support is likely to be offered in these situations, but it will not be without conditions that ensure that the reputation of the family and collective are maintained and that confrontation is avoided (Haj-Yahia & Sadan, 2008). Some of these reflections on the influences of power and relationship do not differ substantially from the feminist ideas of The Stone Centre and others (for example, Gilligan, 1982; Jordan et al., 1991) who have identified the more relational focus of many women and the ways that those with more power may be drawn to privilege autonomy more so than those who are more marginalized in a society (Markus & Kitayama, 1994).

Family members' migration and acculturation status may affect the degree of their allegiance and attachment to the collective. More recent immigrants may have a greater sense of their ethnic group collective, while more settled members of collective cultural communities may feel able to access both the resources of the collective and services in the broader community with which they are familiar. Similarly, and perhaps based on age at the time of migration, there may be diversity within a family with respect to family members' greater or lesser comfort in accessing resources from the collective or dominant society. Employment, housing stability, language fluency, and knowledge of the majority culture, as well as specific community factors such as available services, will all influence the relationship between a person and the minority and majority cultural communities. In addition, for racialized immigrant communities, the influences of systemic racism and intersections with gender, class, and age can contribute to isolation or silencing that increases risk and vulnerability (Jiwani, 2005). These intersections (Sokoloff, 2008) of social and geographic location, as well as aspects of mobility and previous experiences of violence or trauma, will contribute to an individual's choices about where to go for support and what to do in response to that help (Kanagartnam et al., 2012; Yoishioka & Choi, 2005).

Pre-migration Trauma and Family Violence

Families who migrate from conflict or disaster zones have more complex challenges than might be expected from the conventional migration experience. These challenges can influence family members' views of themselves as well as their interpersonal relationships with immediate and extended family, and within minority cultural groups associated with their ethnicity, country of origin, and religious or cultural reference groups, including relationships with people from the dominant culture.

Pre-migration trauma is defined as a person's direct experience, or indirect experience through a close family member, of traumatic events such as murder, rape, torture, or abduction during the pre-migration period. These events may occur within a war zone or refugee camp. Indirect experience may include witnessing these situations or learning about them after the fact from family members.

A study conducted by Baobaid (2008) identified that no specific programs have been developed to date for intervention around family violence in the context of family migration. Pre- and post-migration traumatic experiences can affect individual and relational well-being and health in families. While not examined extensively, we expect that the rate of family violence among families migrating from conflict zones could be notably higher than for other migrant families. Post-traumatic Stress Disorder (PTSD) symptoms of individual family members coming from conflict zones are especially predictive of family distress, loneliness, and severe physical violence.

It is estimated that 48–54% of immigrant populations in Canada and the US report pre-migration political violence exposure (Rousseau & Drapeau, 2004; Eisenman, Gelberg, & Shapiro, 2003). Despite the high rates of intimate partner violence (IPV) among some immigrant groups (Raj & Silverman, 2002; Dutton, Orloff, & Hass, 2000) very little research has been conducted to investigate the relationship between pre-migration trauma and IPV perpetration. The findings of more recent research looking at young adult men attending community health centres in Boston indicated that IPV perpetration was significantly associated with pre-migration exposure to political violence (Gupta et al., 2009). Most refugees present with a combination of both trauma and grief symptoms. These symptoms can be expressed at an individual, family, or community level (Bowles, 2001).

Culturally Integrated Family Safety Response in Practice

MRCSSI in London, Ontario, a mid-sized Canadian city, has used the CIFSR as a basis for several programs oriented to improving prevention and intervention in the area of family violence in the local Muslim community. MRCSSI has developed and implemented unique and innovative responses to effectively reduce risk of family violence, across a continuum, in families coming from collectivist backgrounds, primarily Muslim and Arab families.

It is often the case that those who are experiencing family violence in local minority collectivist communities are not known by established service providers in the broader community during the early stages of family conflict and escalation of family violence. The secrecy around these family circumstances can be understood in the context of collectivism and migration. Family and local community members might provide support in ways that further isolate family members from established services in the broader community. Service providers, when they do become involved, may provide responses that are not viewed as culturally appropriate.

Following the CIFSR model (shown in Figure 2.1), MRCSSI, as a local cultural organization, serves as a hub or cultural broker to link, inform, and support various service providers (for example, child protection, courts,

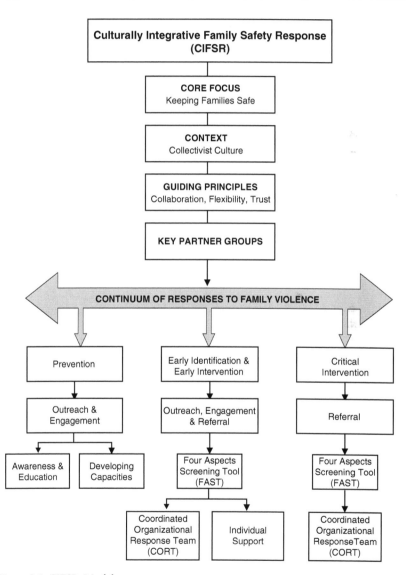

Figure 2.1 CIFSR Model

police, victim services, immigrant services, and healthcare providers) and the local collectivist community. Building bridges between the service provider and local Muslim community has included not only initiating and maintaining relationships, but also educating and supporting both groups. In this way, established services in the broader community can be brought into a more collaborative way of operating across agencies and sectors. And similarly, the strengths and potential supports within the local collectivist Muslim community can be activated to work in tandem with service providers and family members in prevention, early intervention, and longer term support for Muslim families struggling with violence. We note here that the local community we refer to (in London, Ontario), while loosely identifying with a range of adherence to Muslim faith as part of their identity, is an ethnically diverse community comprised of newcomers and settled members. It is a group that is strongly influenced by collectivist values, traditions, and practices. The MRCSSI experience is, we believe, instructive and transferable to other local cultural groups who are primarily collectivist in nature.

Under the CIFSR model, the cultural organization or broker (in this case MRCSSI) works pre-emptively and responsively to build bridges with service providers and the local community. As a first and ongoing step, MRCSSI builds relationships with key service providers and agencies separate and apart from specific families needing support or intervention. These relationships require time and attention, conversations about the local community, potential training opportunities with supervisors or frontline staff, and a commitment to getting to know each other in the context of a long-term relationship. Similarly, identifying potential allies, elders, and mentors in the local community is an important relationship building step. These people will serve in the longer term to enhance preventative efforts and augment collective support for family members in need. A similar but more specific set of relationships is organized around each unique family that is at risk or has become involved with services such as child protection, police or court, or intimate partner violence programs for victims and/or offenders. While some of these services may be mandated by policy or law, other services may be invited into the collaborating group of service providers needed to ensure holistic support that considers short- and longer-term interventions.

Establishing and promoting dialogue between respective cultural communities and established anti-violence services facilitates an environment of mutual understanding and trust, supporting the collaborative development of prevention and intervention materials, resources, and services. Engaging service providers early, before their involvement is mandated, may allow more flexibility of response. For example, engaging a police officer or child protection worker prior to a critical event can allow the family to receive vital information that may avert a crisis. Early involvement may also allow the mandated service provider enhanced knowledge about the family situation that can shape future interventions inviting the collaboration of cultural community members.

Engagement when there is a critical incident is dependent on the mandated service provider's conditions of involvement in regards to the safety of the victim, which is often dictated by law and court. Nevertheless, MRCSSI, in the role of coordinating a culturally integrative response, engages mandated service providers in a team approach and works with them in collaboration, providing tools of engagement that allow for culturally informed pathways of support and intervention to ensure better outcomes. Knowledge of the local community allows MRCSSI to engage religious and cultural community leaders within the team when needed to support the mandated service provider. By involving and supporting community leaders, MRCSSI also develops their capacity and awareness to support at-risk families more generally.

When working with a family guided by this model, it is important to engage all family members where possible, and to take into account absent (either through recent death or through forced separation due to migration complexities) family members. For example, an adolescent daughter may be affected by her mother's pre-migration experience of rape, and/or a father may have been unable to accompany the family to the current host nation as he has received landed immigrant status in another country or continent. Preventative, early, and later interventions also include attention to men who have been abusive, providing necessary supports as a vital part of reducing isolation and risk with the goal of increasing the safety of women, children, and the whole family.

Assessment guidelines are developed within the context of CIFSR for use in all of the programs of MRCSSI. The Four Aspects Screening Tool (FAST) is utilized to augment other commonly used evidence-based assessment practices of service providers in order to identify unique sources for risk of family violence within collectivist immigrant and newcomer communities. The four aspects that are its focus include: ethno-cultural, migration experience, religiosity and faith, and universal aspects. These assessment guidelines and practices are described more fully in Chapter 4.

The team approach advocated by CIFSR includes four major stakeholders (or groups of stakeholders) that make up what is referred to as the Coordinated Organizational Response Team (CORT):

- Cultural Organizations – building bridges and enhancing capacity of service providers and community leaders, as well as fostering open communication amongst stakeholders.
- Service-providing Organizations – mandated or voluntary, will differ according to unique circumstances of each family and presenting concerns.
- Community Support Networks – local cultural community members and organizations – for example, religious/cultural organizations, community leaders, elders, imams – providing informal support to family members.
- Coordinating Organizations – taking responsibility for facilitating overall process of service provision – will differ depending on needs and available resources.

The CORT's core focus is the safety, well-being, and protection of the family with regard to family violence. The general goals are capacity building for the service providers and community members involved, prevention of family violence, and cultural responsiveness. For specific programs, such as the MRCSSI Shared Journeys project that involves child protection agencies, there may be additional goals such as reducing the number of children in care.

CIFSR places high value on open and consistent communication between stakeholders and with family members, adaptability, trust, collaboration, and engagement. The level of engagement by participants in the CORT can be considered along a continuum from informal consultation and advocacy to more formal counselling, support and planning, home visits, and case conferencing. See Chapter 4 for a more detailed description of CORT processes and practices.

CIFSR in Action: Two Case Examples

The following two cases have been adapted from the clinical experience of MRCSSI to highlight the importance of understanding the relevant aspects of the FAST assessment and responding in a culturally integrative way. These case examples, in which MRCSSI served the role of cultural organization, highlight the number of service providers that became involved with the families under the CORT approach, and the community involvement. Each of these stakeholders had independent concerns, perspectives, and solutions for addressing these families' concerns. The following outlines the chronological involvement of service providers with these two families, their varied perspectives, the process of finding common ground, and the outcome. In the interest of confidentiality, the details of cases discussed throughout this book have been altered to protect the identity of MRCSSI clients.

Case Example I: The Influence of Religion (Yasin and Zuhal)

Yasin is a 37-year-old Lebanese Muslim man who has been living in Canada for eight years. He left Lebanon with his uncle and moved to Holland, where he had previously married a Dutch Christian woman. Yasin abandoned his Islamic faith and worship, but did not convert. This marriage eventually ended in divorce and Yasin immigrated to Canada. Since immigrating to Canada, he has recommitted to his Islamic faith. In the past year, Yasin returned to Lebanon, to the village where he was born, in order to remarry. Yasin's father, who lives in Lebanon, is a devout Muslim and is recognized and honoured in his community. Yasin's family strongly supported and encouraged his marriage to a woman from his village, named Zuhal.

Chronological Involvement of Stakeholders/Services

PHYSICIAN

Upon returning to London, Ontario, Yasin and his new wife Zuhal had a baby boy. Zuhal visited the doctor's office for her postpartum medical exam, and during the course of this medical exam she disclosed that Yasin had beaten her. She presented with no physical indicators of abuse and seemed somewhat incoherent to the doctor. However, the doctor was concerned about his obligation to report such disclosures and contacted the police to report the situation.

POLICE

Police, in response to the physician's call, arrived to the doctor's office and interviewed Zuhal. The information she provided appeared contradictory to episodes of violence. Yasin was also questioned and denied any violence toward his wife. The police felt there was more concern with Zuhal's incoherence and the risk that it posed for their son. They felt the best action was to involve the child protection agency.

CHILD PROTECTION AGENCY

After being contacted by the police, the child protection agency ordered a psychiatric assessment for Zuhal. She was diagnosed with postpartum psychosis (with no further involvement of the psychiatrist) and therefore the child protection agency considered her unable to be alone with her child. The family had a friend living with them and supporting them, which allowed the baby to stay home. However, there came a time when this friend was not able to stay with the family, and given Yasin's long work hours, the child protection agency determined that it was no longer acceptable for the child to stay in the home.

The issue of intimate partner abuse was still on everyone's radar. After receiving the initial call, the intake worker referred the case to MRCSSI (see below), and there was debate within the child protection agency regarding which internal team would assume the responsibility for the case: the family violence team or the diversity team. The diversity team ended up taking the lead as a result of consultation with MRCSSI. The child protection agency still felt it necessary to address any possible family violence and contacted the local public health team, given their typical involvement in situations involving infants.

PUBLIC HEALTH TEAM

As indicated above, when child protection agencies are involved with families of infants, the public health nurse is typically part of the team of service providers and conducts home visits. The public health team became very focused on protocol in the area of intimate partner abuse given their perceptions of the religiosity of the family and the young age of the infant. The team expressed a shared level of concern that Yasin looked like a "religious fundamentalist," in that he had a long beard and demonstrated what the service providers saw as controlling behaviour. It became necessary, due to the concerns of the public health team, to require a conference at the child protection agency that included the manager of the family violence program. It was important at this conference to review the risk factors and get the support of the child protection agency, in order to move forward and alleviate some of the concerns of the public health team. This conference was attended by the child protection agency's diversity supervisor with the representation of MRCSSI through internal conferencing. It was determined at that point that the family violence director from the child protection agency would need to become aware of and support the work of MRCSSI and the diversity team, while recognizing the public health concerns. All future case conferences were attended by the child protection agency's diversity team, public health, and MRCSSI. This was an example of supporting and encouraging some involvement outside of the strict mandate of the child protection agency while supporting and encouraging the public health team to begin to view this family and the couple's relationship in a different light. The intervention that was engaged through internal case conferencing allowed for some level of support to carry forward the work between the diversity team at the child protection agency and MRCSSI. Many sessions and conferences occurred between public health, the child protection agency, and MRCSSI, which resulted in educating the service providers about cultural differences and concerns for family violence.

MRCSSI

Once approached by the intake worker from the child protection agency, MRCSSI was able to engage with the family in a number of unique ways. Two months into the work of supporting this family, the supportive person in the family home was expecting to go away on vacation for six to eight weeks. Because Yasin was working and Zuhal was unable to care for the child on her own, MRCSSI became involved in arranging kinship care for the child. Placing the child within the faith community was very important for both Yasin and Zuhal. A kinship family, approved by the child protection agency and known to MRCSSI, was able to provide support and safety not only for the baby, but also for Zuhal. She was able to visit daily and develop a bond with her child, while overcoming her battle with postpartum psychosis. Her family doctor was involved in care, and over time with continued contact with her child on a daily basis she began to feel more competent as a parent. MRCSSI was also engaged with her and with Yasin to ensure parental continuity and support. Yasin was engaged in taking a more active role and Zuhal's postpartum psychosis was eventually alleviated.

MRCSSI was also able to work with the family in the area of faith, which the other service providers were not comfortable addressing themselves. MRCSSI was able to invite the local imam to discuss with the family the Islamic way of treating one another and raising their son. The focus of the imam was on gender equality in Islam and the collective responsibility of both parents toward raising the child, rather than seeing childrearing as the mother's sole responsibility. Yasin indicated that he felt supported by the imam and the male staff that he connected with at MRCSSI. He became more engaged and responsible as a parent, reducing the demands on Zuhal and allowing her to also become more engaged in responding to the needs of their child.

Impact and Outcomes

Finding a way for the child protection agency and public health to work together, alongside the involvement of imam and MRCSSI counsellors, resulted in the attainment of common goals of family safety while also reuniting this family. These attitudinal shifts at the organizational level can also be described as positive outcomes of the CIFSR-guided interventions. Yasin, Zuhal, and their son were all supported in a way that kept them connected to one another, their community, and their religion. The son was returned to their family home once the in-home supportive person returned from vacation. Both parents had adjusted their responsibilities, with Yasin becoming more involved and Zuhal feeling more competent and not having to bear the full responsibility for their son's upbringing. Zuhal and her son developed a strong bond, and currently the family is happy and healthy. They have also recently been blessed with their second child, who is also healthy and happy.

This example shows how using the CIFSR model supports a better outcome in responding to complex cases like this. Usually if infants are involved the case becomes high risk and the child protection agency's family violence team takes the lead. In that event, the focus becomes primarily paying attention to evidence that the woman and her the child are at risk of being subjected to family violence. In this case, because trust was already built between the child protection agency and MRCSSI, the process was slowed down and MRCSSI's opinion was given more prominence. MRCSSI's engagement meant that the child protection agency was able to consider different ways of responding to the complex situation with positive outcomes that met the mandates of the various agencies involved as well as the needs of the family.

Case Example II: The Influence of Culture (Zuhair)

Zuhair was a 17-year-old young man who journeyed to Canada from the Middle East with his mother and younger sister. His father was resettled in a European country. Although they had been separated for over two years,

Zuhair still communicated with his father during the time period described here. His father had made it clear to Zuhair that he was to be the "man of the house" until a future point when he would be able to reunite with the family. This cultural pressure on the oldest male in the home had created friction in the home.

Chronological Involvement of Stakeholders/Services

POLICE

After four months of being in Canada, Zuhair and his mother got into an altercation. Zuhair threw a small object in his mother's direction in anger. Wanting assistance from male authority figures who could speak with her son and convince him to listen to her, Zuhair's mother contacted the police. The police investigated the situation and according to their policies and procedures, charged Zuhair with the assault of his mother. He was issued a restraining order and encouraged to go to a local men's shelter. The police family consultants became involved and they felt it appropriate to connect with MRCSSI, especially surrounding the living accommodations for Zuhair. Usually the police family consultants work with families involved with violence and provide the support needed for the victims, while also supporting the family in finding resources and supports that would enable them to overcome stressors that could lead to violence. They also felt it necessary to engage the youth therapeutic court team, a team typically involved when a charged youth and his family are involved in a conflict and the justice system.

MRCSSI

MRCSSI became involved after the reported episode of violence occurred, at the request of the police family consultants. When approached, MRCSSI was able to engage the agencies involved for a CORT response. This included the local settlement agency, the Crown (prosecutor) assigned to prosecuting this case, Zuhair's lawyer, and the imam. MRCSSI counsellors were able to inform Zuhair of the risk factors that could impact family safety and the potential positive and negative effects that his responses might have on him as well as his family. MRCSSI was also able to place Zuhair in a kinship home approved by the child protection agency, keeping him away from the shelter experience and the risks associated with homelessness. This also allowed him to stay engaged in the community and build support networks for the future.

MRCSSI was able to identify the potential dynamics of honour-based conflict escalation. There was a great deal of conflict between Zuhair's mother and sister. They understood Zuhair's role of being the father-like figure in his father's absence, which was being promoted by both parents. The daughter had been engaging in behaviours that were not welcomed or approved by her mother, including staying outside their home until late at night and hanging out with older female friends of whom the mother did not approve, placing stress on her mother and more pressure on Zuhair.

MRCSSI was able to provide counselling services for the young man and his mother as well as coordinating with the rest of the CORT team including the youth therapeutic court team. This ensured that everyone who was involved in this case would be informed about the cultural context of the family interactions and relationships, and provided the family with culturally responsive service. They were able to clearly identify challenges and risk factors, tailor services and communicate needs to the other service providers.

COURT

Over several months, MRCSSI was able to educate Zuhair's lawyer about the need for a differential response. This allowed the Crown (prosecutor) and then the judge to refer the situation to the youth therapeutic court, and to utilize the youth therapeutic court team as Zuhair was just under the age of 18. Differential response means, in this context, that the focus is more on the socio-cultural context of the situation rather than only looking at criminal justice facts.

SETTLEMENT AGENCY

The settlement worker, who spoke the same language and held similar cultural beliefs as Zuhair and his family, had a much stricter perspective than other CORT members. The settlement worker believed that there should be a harsh consequence for this young man's behaviour. The worker felt that it would be good for Zuhair to learn his lesson with no leeway or exception. The settlement worker expressed little desire to engage in a differential response or consider the complexity of the issues that Zuhair and his family faced. As a result, the CORT focused on finding a suitable placement alternative rather than engaging this particular settlement worker. Later CORT meetings engaged representation from the settlement agency, and they did not select this original worker to be part of the process.

Impact and Outcomes

With the engagement of all the service providers surrounding the safety of not just mother, sister, or Zuhair, but rather the whole family unit, they were able to meet the needs of the family and promote positive change for all involved. The absent father unfortunately died in a refugee camp, so reconciliation efforts were directed at Zuhair, his sister, and mother. Various services became involved in making this family stronger and healthier, including the court system, the crown attorney, and the lawyers. The unique services provided to this family could be seen in the early identification of risk factors that were identified by MRCSSI through using the FAST tool. MRCSSI counsellors were able to focus more on the migration journey of the family as well as the cultural differences. MRCSSI was able to build a strong foundation for better understanding the context of the lived reality of the family and assessing the risk in its cultural context through engaging with relevant service providers early on. The interventions used in this case by all the members of the CORT process were culturally informed, with a positive outcome and a result that ensured the safety of the victim while respecting and understanding the family. There was a significant impact of understanding the family's pre-migration concerns, the absence of Zuhair's father, and the intergenerational conflict.

The joint support of the CORT process supported this family to prevent further escalation of violence. The extra steps taken by the police as well as the court prevented a much worse situation for this family. There was potential for escalation of honour-related violence. The mother's guilt was significantly reduced, as was the blame that was placed on her by both her daughter and son. Zuhair's traumatic experiences were kept to a minimum by using a culturally appropriate alternative to staying in a shelter and supporting him throughout the court process, thus reducing the risk of further violence in the family. It was also a positive learning experience for Zuhair's mother and the rest of the family, as they became more aware of the services available to them and the consequences of using violence or physical expressions of anger.

What community service providers have to say...

"For me, it [team of service providers] was very helpful because I could see I'm not alone. And I can ask for help and I'm asking the right person for that and it's very easy to coordinate, to avoid, as [name] said, duplication. So, we save time and we get more results, and in a very short time. Also, I found it an opportunity to understand my client more from different perspectives."

(Service provider, Safe Integration Project)

"The first one [team meeting] I went to, they had eco-maps and they used genograms and those typical tools aren't used that much in the immigration field. So, kind of bringing a little of that professionalism into and understanding from those tools more of the clients' situations, the relationships, how systems interplay with that family and in terms of education, immigration, mental health, medical, everything, just seeing how those things work together and influence one another."

(Settlement worker, Safe Integration Project)

"At some point everyone realized this family has only been here since September. They're exactly where they should be. Why are we rushing? The problem is what's around the family rather than what's in the family. And if we're not exactly where the family wants us to be then how are we helping them?"

(Community worker, Safe Integration Project)

3 Building Connections – Training, Capacity Building, and Prevention

The Culturally Integrative Family Safety Response (CIFSR) model coordinates supports around families and service agencies to increase safety and decrease risk on all levels of a violence and conflict continuum (see Figure 3.1). This holistic approach reflects a corresponding continuum of responses that include prevention, early identification and early intervention, and critical intervention approaches. Prevention strategies, described in this chapter, aim to stop family violence before it occurs. CIFSR-guided collaborative efforts are directed at shifting attitudes, perceptions, and behaviours of families, communities, and existing services, as well as building capacity and creating strategies to end family violence. Further along the response continuum, early identification and interventions, discussed in more detail in Chapter 4, respond to family situations before they escalate and require mandated service involvement (e.g., child protection). At the far end of the violence and response continuums, critical interventions, as described in Chapter 5, refer to more complex situations with high risk to family members' safety.

In this chapter, we describe CIFSR prevention efforts at the level of communities and organizations, as well as with individual families. We present the early and ongoing steps of building relationships and connections between established service providers in the broader community and the local collectivist community identified by ethno-cultural or religious roots. This early work sets the stage for culturally integrative interventions through preparing both communities to work together. It includes community outreach, developing capacity for attending to family safety with community leaders and local champions for family safety, and capacity for working within a collectivist context with service providers in the broader community. We discuss some of the challenges that can attend training and capacity building across these distinct organizational and social cultures. Further, we present the earliest of interventions with individual families, primarily preventative responses.

Increasing Awareness and Initiating Partnerships in Communities and Organizations

At a broad community level, increased awareness and opportunities for preventative interventions are evident early on in the process of establishing

Culturally Integrative Family Safety Response Engagement Continuum

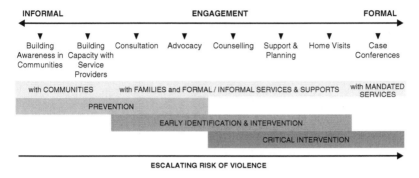

Figure 3.1 CIFSR Engagement Continuum

a CIFSR partnership. Such a partnership can be initiated by any of the key stakeholders, service-providing organizations, cultural organizations, or interested and engaged community members. As these various individuals and groups share knowledge about family safety and risks of family violence, they become more informed about formal and informal resources, build relationships with each other as persons and organizations interested in keeping families safe, and become aware of gaps between or misperceptions about groups and services that can be addressed. In itself, the act of building a collaborative group of formal and informal supports for family safety provides opportunities for prevention and awareness. Furthermore, once a CIFSR partnership is established in a community, there are opportunities to use this model to guide support for individual families in the context of their communities and address situations of risk or concern early on.

As illustrated in the previous chapter (Figure 2.1), the CIFSR model is grounded in a core focus on family safety and making central the perspectives and needs of families who are experiencing or are at risk of experiencing family violence.

The expected outcomes of the CIFSR model include:

- Service providers with enhanced knowledge of the cultural context and needs of families in collectivist communities.
- Cultural communities with increased knowledge and understanding of established service-providing organizations' mandates.
- Service providers engaged in supporting safety at early stages of family conflict prior to critical events.
- Established organizations with increased capacity for responding to the complex needs of families in collectivist cultural communities.
- Reduced gaps between the needs of marginalized cultural communities and the services of established organizations in the broader community.
- Enhanced collaborative and culturally integrative responses to family violence.

Collective Prevention Measures

Broad community engagement in collective responsibility, respect, and support for those who are struggling in marginalized communities is at the forefront of the partnership guided by the CIFSR model. Early discussions between potential partners and key stakeholders are focused on how best to meet the shared goal of keeping families safe, and the work of all of these organizations is directed on a continuum of intervention that includes prevention, i.e., stopping family violence before it occurs. The CIFSR model considers prevention in the context of a collaborative group of service providers and community partners, and how knowledge held within professional, organizational, or cultural boundaries can be shared and extended to the broader community. Collaborative efforts are directed at shifting attitudes, perceptions, and behaviours for families, communities, and established services. As communities engage with each other in prevention and outreach, they increase their knowledge and awareness of issues of violence and safety, and collectively create strategies for ensuring family safety.

Prevention responses enhance the capacities of all of the partners involved. For example, in 2003 when war was declared in Iraq, the local child protection agency sent out a letter to foster parents designed to help them talk to foster children about the war with a prime directive to reassure children that the war was far away and would not have a direct impact on their lives. At this time, 10% of the children in their care had their origins in the Middle East. Of course, this advice for foster parents in such a context was misguided. The openness of the agency to addressing this initial lack of cultural awareness, through a letter to the local mosques, demonstrated their ability to hear their partners and to share their new knowledge with immediate response.

Prevention measures within a CIFSR-guided approach include engaging community members as agents of anti-violence education; for example, inviting religious leaders and local champions to share information about family violence with others in their community. In addition to educating community leaders about warning signs of family violence and their obligation to support those who would be most vulnerable to family violence, facilitators of these discussions are also interested in inviting them to think about how they can be more sensitive to the needs of those who are at risk of becoming victims of family violence. These facilitators also assist local leaders in the community in considering how they can use their moral authority as an effective means of changing community attitudes toward victims and perpetrators of family violence.

In addition to future participation in individual response teams working with families who are at risk of or experiencing family violence, the CIFSR group of partner organizations and community members will remain active in ongoing preventative work across the divide of existing service-providing organizations and less well-established, newcomer, or marginalized ethnocultural communities. These initiatives work to inform all of those involved about the resources, risks, and realities of the local communities, as well as the intentions and initiatives of established organizations in the broader community to promote family safety.

Prevention can move beyond simply sharing knowledge and information through active engagement in developing and extending capacities. For established service providers this can include enhanced cultural competence and understanding. Local community members can extend their skills and support others to identify signs of safety or risk in relationships, to reduce isolation, and to mentor and support parents and their children in resolving conflict safely.

The organization that champions and initiates the use of this model in a particular location takes leadership in bringing together, building bridges, and responding to community dialogues and discourses about specific local communities and family violence. These early and continued conversations and the actions that emerge from them provide preventative measures to keep families safe, both in the local collectivist community and amongst the broader population. These early preventative measures are augmented over time by the increased number of partner organizations, culturally informed and experienced service providers, local allies, and mentors.

Building Capacity and Partnerships with Communities and Service Providers

The context of families who are residing in collectivist communities and hold collectivist ethno-cultural values is a key component of the CIFSR model. In addition to the ethno-cultural backdrop, we note that the current context for the families with whom the Muslim Resource Centre for Social Support and Integration (MRCSSI) works is that they are primarily newcomers (both refugees and immigrants) and that many have been exposed to pre-migration trauma as a result of having lived in conflict zones for some period of time. As described earlier, the success of CIFSR is contingent on understanding the dilemmas that prevent family members in this context, in particular women and children who are being abused, from seeking outside help. Capacity building for service providers includes training and learning through participating in CIFSR-directed teams and attending to the influence of various contextual factors on family members' behaviours, interactions with others, and understanding of current circumstances.

The guiding principles that support a range of responses from all stakeholders include flexibility, collaboration, and trust. Some service provider organizations have less flexibility with regard to their mandate and governance, whereas others may have greater flexibility. A willingness to work alongside informal support persons allows for a more flexible and collaborative response. Best outcomes for families are more likely when there are multiple partners who engage in knowledge sharing, learning from each other, and capacity building. A collaborative structure of service delivery allows for a response to families that surrounds them (see Figure 3.2), perhaps more in keeping

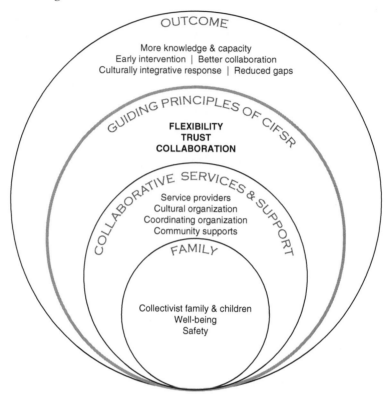

Figure 3.2 Building Capacity and Partnerships with Communities and Service Providers

with collectivist principles. Working across traditional boundaries, being more flexible, and making a commitment to collaborative ways of working requires trust between service partners. This is especially true when the stakes are high in terms of safety, confidentiality, and the sensitive nature of these family situations. Trust building and strengthening these types of relationships between organizations, individual service providers, and engaged members of the local community requires time and often starts with engaging in dialogue, preferably before there is a specific concern, and debriefing after a collaborative CIFSR-guided response. One of the key ingredients for this type of collaborative work is time spent in relationship building. Including a culturally based organization in these efforts to build relationships and partnerships does require more time than more traditional partnership building between established services only. We believe this time is well spent early in the process of preventing violence and working toward more effective interventions to keep families safe.

The key partners for a local CIFSR initiative include a coordinating organization, formal service-providing organizations, and leaders, anti-violence champions, and informal ethno-cultural or religious organizations in the local community. These key partner groups can cover a range of participants from multiple service sectors and informal supports. Together, the group of key partners forms a collaborative structure of service delivery focused on supporting families in need. The formation of a partnership of organizations in a particular community will involve the first step of discussing shared aims and objectives in moving forward with the CIFSR model. These conversations should include members of the local cultural community as well as a broad range of service-providing organizations – including, for example, immigrant settlement, child protection, housing, family violence, court, police, victims support services, education, health, and social service sectors. Reaching more formal partnership agreements or memoranda of understanding will ensure clarity with regard to commitment to the CIFSR model and expected outcomes.

Following on these agreements, and beyond prevention initiatives, appropriate personnel from partner organizations will serve on future case-specific response teams, and these teams will also include informal supports and family members. The partnership may be organized such that one organization will take on the coordinating role for these future individual response teams fairly consistently, or this may be delegated to what is deemed the most appropriate service-providing organization depending on mandates for services and the presenting concerns of the family.

The coordinating organization has primary responsibility for acting as a bridge, broker, or connector for the various partner organizations and individuals, in order to facilitate their engagement in the collaborative response to the family in need. It may be that there is a coordinating organization that takes on a leadership and facilitative role early in the formation of a collaborative group of organizations and individuals for working within the CIFSR model in a particular community. As individual families in need are supported using this model, this organization may serve consistently in the role of developing and facilitating the teams of formal and informal supports established for each unique family. The specific constellation of response teams will vary depending on the nature of a specific set of circumstances and the needs of the family involved. For example, a particular instance may call for involvement of immigration, school, and court systems together with a group of family members, a leader from the local mosque, and a small group of community members who are knowledgeable in the area of parenting adolescents. Another situation may call for partners within child protection services and a women's shelter, together with carefully chosen family members and community mentors.

The CIFSR model designates these teams as Coordinated Organizational Response Teams (CORT) and we describe them in more detail in Chapter 4. In our experience, for example, MRCSSI (the local cultural organization) provided the impetus for developing these practices and engaging a range of service providers and community members. Currently, MRCSSI also takes the coordinating role of developing and facilitating individual responses that engage the group of involved service providers (unless a mandated service is already working with a family, in which case that organization coordinates case conferences, and a concurrent CORT process may inform the case conference on an advisory basis). Alternatively, the broader group of involved service providers in a community may determine that any one of several organizations can serve as the CORT coordinating organization. See Chapter 4 for more detail on the structure and function of CORT in response to each unique family's circumstances.

Challenges Associated with Training and Capacity Building

The description of the CIFSR model points to the importance of setting the stage for culturally integrative work through training and capacity building across existing service-provider sectors in the broader community and local collectivist communities. Preparing both communities to work together includes outreach that develops capacity to better understand how collectivist values and family safety intersect with local community leaders and champions, as well as established service providers' frontline workers and organizational leaders. As outlined earlier, there are significant differences between individualist and collectivist societies that are generally not well understood. Without direct lived experience of a collectivist society, a person's perceptions and interpretations of difference will always be experienced through the lens of their own life experience. This means that there will be a limit to full comprehension and understanding of differences. What we aim to promote is an appreciation and respect, not only for this diversity, but also for the challenges and imperatives associated with maintaining dialogue and inter- action in the face of never-fully-resolved-or-understood differences. In keeping with the concept of cultural humility (Tervalon & Murray-Garcia, 1998), accepting and appreciating values and ideas that are not part of our own experience are at the heart of this dialogue and collective learning.

Working within the CIFSR model also requires considerable time and energy devoted by all partners to building and sustaining relationships. This can be challenging and, ultimately, very rewarding. While this is a strength of the model, we recognize that justifying the resources allocated to relationship building will not always be easy, particularly in an organizational context that has not traditionally placed value on these activities. It is a different way of working for some, and an opportunity to enrich more individualistic practices with those that are more collectively oriented. In addition to providing for more holistic and effective support for the safety of families in collectivist communities, we consider that these practices may also enhance organizational and community-wide partnerships and services. As we mentioned earlier in this section, CIFSR partnerships rest on guiding principles that include collabora- tion, flexibility, and trust. Practicing these principles requires careful and frequent communication, openness, and transparency, alongside a willingness to discuss potentially difficult or contentious issues and a commitment to constructively addressing areas of conflict with respect. Relationship building is central to supporting these skills and attributes of successful community partnerships. Such initiatives may appear to be challenging in the current context of financial cutbacks and reduced services in publicly funded agencies. It may be, however, that the investment in relationship building and prevention work at the community level will also provide opportunities for creatively and more effectively enhancing family safety and supporting the service providers who are engaged in this work.

Family-level Prevention

In addition to organization- and community-level prevention in the form of outreach and capacity building, early identification of families who are at risk of suffering from family violence provides opportunities for preventative engagement at the family level. Family violence within collectivist families and communities is often shrouded in secrecy, making it difficult for service providers more familiar with working within the mainstream culture to identify abuse and respond accordingly. The private nature of family violence and the foreignness of the concept of family violence within most collectivist cultures will often preclude children and family members from divulging family secrets. Although service providers may be unaware of abuse, community members and community leaders may know of or suspect family violence. During family struggles, families may connect with their imam and/or community elders for advice and guidance. These concerns may centre on conflict and negotiation with children and adolescents who are trying to manage their daily lives at home and school across two very different cultures with often competing norms and directives. Similarly, the dominant culture may introduce new questions for family members about gender norms and expectations, and appropriate means of disciplining or guiding family members' behaviour within a framework of gender equality.

In order to gain access to families who may be on the threshold of physical violence toward girls and young women who are perceived as disobeying or dishonouring their family, a partnership with organizations who have trusting relationships with cultural and faith groups provides established service providers with a bridge to the minority or marginalized cultural community. Building trusting relationships between existing services and cultural groups can result in increased referrals from community and faith leaders and make possible early identification of risk and intervention to enhance safety. Community engagement strategies also include outreach to families in natural gathering places. These gathering places may include mosques, cultural centres, and settlement services. Through education and awareness messages, community groups and families may become more familiar with offered supports and may be more likely to seek out services themselves.

Early engagement with families at the stage where they are looking for solutions and supports may lead to early identification of potential family violence and more effective responses to ensure safety. It is unlikely that these initial contacts with service providers will be framed as a problem with family violence. Such concerns are more likely to be presented by family members, parents, or spouses as related to mental health concerns, legal problems, and guidance (for children to obey their parents, or wives to respect their husbands). These requests for assistance may be directed to teachers, family doctors, settlement workers, or employment or social assistance workers. Regardless of how families name the presenting problems and to whom they direct their request, it is important that the service provider's response is timely and engages them in ways that make sense to them based on their understanding of the problem. This helps set the stage for establishing the nature and origin of conflicts and where they are positioned along the continuum of family violence.

Family-level prevention strategies and early identification and intervention responses can be carried out by a coordinating organization or shared by the CIFSR-guided collaborative group of organizations and individuals. These strategies consist of the following elements:

- Identify vulnerable and at-risk individuals and families through community and individual engagement strategies.
- Reach out to diverse groups in the community and raise awareness of warning signs for family violence, as well as available resources for family support.
- Train individuals from diverse cultural communities to act as cultural brokers, bridging established services in the broader community and the local collectivist community.
- Engage community leaders and established service providers in discussing barriers to service and developing creative solutions that help potential victims overcome barriers of asking for help.

CIFSR Prevention and Early Intervention: Three Case Examples

We provide here two examples of CIFSR-guided community outreach and prevention initiatives. We also present a case example of what we consider to be a positive early intervention with a family. As with all of our presented case examples, the family intervention is presented with names and some details changed in order to protect confidentiality.

Case Example I: Building a Relationship (Children's Aid Society of London and Middlesex and MRCSSI)

In 2003, the Muslim Family Safety Project (MFSP) was established (and later evolved into the current MRCSSI) to build mutual understanding between the London Muslim community and the anti-violence community in London, Ontario. The Children's Aid Society of London and Middlesex (CASLM) was one of the key organizations engaged in this project. Through this project the Muslim community leaders and CASLM were involved in an informal relationship. It opened opportunities to raise awareness of child protection issues through the mosques and also to train child protection workers on the cultural context of family dynamics within Muslim communities. This informal relationship also allowed us to contribute to addressing some complex cases involving Muslim parents struggling with their teenage daughters who had decided to leave their family homes. These situations had created some tension and, in some cases, real crises between respective Muslim families, the Muslim community, and CASLM. When MRCSSI was established in 2009 as a continuation of the MFSP, the relationship between MRCSSI and CASLM was formalized. Both partner agencies had learned from their previous relationship and experiences and, out of this learning, prepared a protocol of understanding as well as practical mechanisms to work collaboratively in prevention, early intervention, and critical intervention with local Muslim families.

This collaborative partnership was designed to develop culturally appropriate responses to the complex needs of Muslim families involved with CASLM. The collaboration had a significant impact in reducing the number of Muslim children in care. Beginning in 2012, across three consecutive years, no Muslim child entered care within the area serviced by CASLM (while prior to this these numbers fluctuated, there were, for example, 26 Muslim children in care in 2007 and 11 Muslim children in care in 2009). This partnership also contributed to developing the capacity of the local Muslim community with regard to addressing family violence against children, recognizing early warning signs of violence, and supporting families to access services to address issues before a critical event occurred that would result in the involvement of mandated service providers. In addition, the protocol of understanding ensured that any Muslim family who was involved with CASLM would be referred to MRCSSI for supportive counselling services if they were willing. This collaboration helped the child protection workers to more effectively engage with Muslim families and surface cultural community resources to support more positive outcomes. In collaboration, CASLM and MRCSSI were able to jointly recruit volunteers and kinship families from the Muslim community to meet the needs of local Muslim children and families. The capacity of the local Muslim community to respond to situations of families at risk was greatly enhanced through this collaboration.

As a result of the success of this partnership, provincial funding was provided to MRCSSI to transfer this model of collaboration to other Ontario cities through a project entitled the Shared Journeys Project. The areas involved in the Shared Journeys Project included the Ontario communities of: Kingston, through the Islamic Society of Kingston and Family and Children's Services of Frontenac, Lennox, and Addington; Ottawa, through the Children's Aid Society of Ottawa and Muslim Family Services of

Ottawa; and York Region, through the York Region Children's Aid Society and the Social Service Network of Markham. The programs in Kingston and Ottawa focused principally on the engagement of the child protection agencies with local Muslim community organizations. In York Region, the program has centred on developing the partnership between child protection services and the local South Asian community.

The outcome of the Shared Journeys Project is enhanced training, connections, and formalizing relationships between partnered agencies in each of these communities. The collaborations initiated as part of the Shared Journeys Project are continuing. In York Region the project has been extended to include more than 26 community-based organizations including organizations serving immigrants as well as other social and anti-violence agencies. They have established a joint advisory committee and adapted the MRCSSI CASLM protocol of understanding. In Ottawa, Muslim Family Services and the Children's Aid Society (CAS) have strengthened community engagement and recruited more Muslim foster families, as well as enhancing supports for Muslim families with children involved with CAS. In Kingston, the partnership has included other multicultural communities, in particular the Latino community, and they remain committed to continue working together in the spirit of the Shared Journeys Project. MRCSSI is continuing working with other partners in the province, primarily focused on initiating conversations between large local Muslim community organizations and associated regional child protection agencies, and providing training in the CIFSR model.

In describing contemporary not-for-profit organizations and the value of building unexpected partnerships with shared interests, Marilyn Struthers (Inaugural John C. Eaton Chair in Social Innovation and Entrepreneurship at Ryerson University, Toronto) drew on MRCSSI's experience:

> For example, what does a children's aid society have in common with a mosque? Answer: a deep concern for children across very different family storylines. I recently had the privilege of working with the Muslim Resource Centre for Social Service and Integration (MRCSSI), one of a new class of 'intermediary organizations.' MRCSSI deliberately brokers the tricky terrain of child welfare by creating multiple connections and then linking and mediating relationships between the Muslim and the child welfare community. Working from common interest, both faith and service communities are providing resources, and their shared commitment leverages the interest of other funders.
>
> (Struthers, 2013)

Case Example II: Community Outreach and Prevention (The Reclaim Honour Project)

MRCSSI received funding from Status of Women Canada in 2013 to initiate a community-based violence prevention project grounded in participatory action principles. Twenty-one young Muslim women (ages 17–24 years), and later, eight young Muslim men (ages 17–24 years), worked as community facilitators to raise awareness and foster community engagement about gender-based and family violence. Early in the project, the group intentionally decided to move away from using "honour-based violence" language due to the stigmatizing and "othering" potential of this language. Instead, the Reclaim Honour project used the more neutral and universal language of "gender-based and family violence" as a reminder that this type of violence occurs in all communities, and to avoid the ways in which reference to honour-based violence may focus on cultural or religion-based explanations of specific forms of violence. The group worked within a contextual and intersectional framework of seeing various forms of gender-based and family violence shaped by socio-cultural contexts and a range of factors and justified in various ways.

The group named the project "Reclaim Honour" with the purpose of:

- Challenging any and all justifications for gender-based and family violence, including justifications of "honour."
- Challenging simplistic and "othering" understandings and impacts of prevailing constructions of gender-based and family violence in Muslim communities and families.
- Exploring the complexities of different forms of gender-based and family violence.
- Honouring the strengths and capacities that exist within girls and women, families, and communities to address issues of gender-based and family violence.

Reclaim Honour community facilitators engaged in their own discussion and process of discovery, and then in community outreach, awareness building, and public education. They facilitated community meetings to name and recognize the issue of gender-based and family violence, to mobilize stakeholders to collaborate and ensure accountability, to create opportunities to meet with young Muslim women, to allow youth to explore these issues using arts-based activities, and to encourage community conversations. They also organized workshops with service providers.

This project had effects at multiple levels – both for the young women and men who participated as community facilitators, and for the members of the community and service providers who participated in the project events. One member of the project team said,

> I have experienced tremendous growth during my time with Reclaim Honour. I feel confident to lead and facilitate conversations about this sensitive topic. I feel confident enough to challenge others to think about the issue through different lenses and to challenge problematic thinking.

Another stated that "It has provided me with inspiration, opportunity, and capacity on how to be a positive agent in addressing issues that affect the community."

Those who attended Reclaim Honour events said:

> In the workshop they gave scenarios and stories. It was a window into women's lives. In those discussions, it helped challenge my biases and stereotypes. What I see as empowerment as a woman may look different for others. It brought new perspective.

> Outside of Reclaim Honour circles, I started to see things in the community I had not noticed before. I was much more aware. I changed my language within my job, based on my involvement in the project.

> It has helped initiate the shift in attitudes, perceptions, and behaviours of families, communities, and hopefully in the future, of mainstream services. This paradigm shift will have significant positive family safety implications for many Muslim families in our community.

> Transformation within the Muslim leadership, I've seen it with my own eyes. Executive directors from other agencies have been inspired by the young women and their approach.

Reclaim Honour helped service providers learn more about the complexities of gender-based and family violence and its many forms. Attention to language and critical consideration of gender-based and family violence provided more opportunities for community conversations, as well as enhanced awareness of complexities for the project facilitators and members of the community. This project also demonstrates the value of involving young people as leaders of community dialogue, the participation of religious leaders and social institutions, and a strengths-based approach to developing community capacity to address this challenging issue. A range of strategies from arts-based messaging, use of social media, panel discussions and keynote speakers, community conversations, and interactive workshops allowed an engagement process that built awareness, developed rapport among community members, and fostered community responsibility for addressing gender-based and family violence.

Case Example III: Early and Preventative Responses to a Family (Amina)

An example of preventative responses at the family level is evident in the case of an abused woman who left her home with her children to stay with a friend. Although Amina had attended the hospital emergency room with bruises, she denied any abuse. The child protection agency did not determine that there was any evidence of child abuse or that the children had been witnesses to violence. As a result, the child protection file was closed. A friend of this family met with an imam and the imam said that intervening in this situation was beyond his professional capacity. The imam encouraged Amina to involve our agency, MRCSSI, as a professional agency, in this conversation. Amina agreed, but also insisted that the conversation not involve the police or any other broader community-based service. She indicated that she did not want to cause any problems for her husband who was physically disabled as a result of torture sustained in his country of origin, from which he had escaped. When MRCSSI staff members met with Amina at the mosque, with the imam present, we tried to help her understand how she and her family, including her husband, could benefit from accessing existing services in the broader community. We suggested to her that reporting what had happened to her would also benefit her husband by facilitating his access to appropriate treatment for the pre-migration trauma he had experienced. In our next meeting at the mosque she agreed to invite a social worker from the police family consultant service.

What stands out here is that this process of engagement allowed the bringing together of the community, mandated services, the family friend, and the victim – all key players in a meeting that had initially seemed nearly impossible. We (MRCSSI staff members involved in the process) believe that one very powerful statement of the imam changed Amina's attitude, as a victim of violence, toward involving established services in the broader community. He said to her,

> Allah trusted you with your body, so you don't allow anybody to hurt you regardless of your relationship to this person. Everyone is accountable before Allah for their deed. This is my religious advice. You need help, your children need help, and your husband needs help. The authorities are here to help us all.

This statement appeared to change everything and after this, the key partners worked very well together with a very positive outcome. MRCSSI asked the child protection agency to reopen the file, and a worker from the women's shelter was also involved. The police family consultants continued to be involved, but in a totally different manner by agreeing to come to the mosque and participating in this meeting with the imam present. All of the participants tried to work with Amina, as a victim of violence, from where she was rather than what others thought she needed to do to be safe. Amina's husband was involved in a counselling program at MRCSSI and also was seen by a psychiatrist through a coordinated response program. The family reconciled and both the husband and the wife went back to English-language classes and continued to receive social and logistical support from some of the local community members including those affiliated with the mosque. At the same time the child protection agency closed the file and was satisfied with the family's safety plan.

What community service providers have to say...

"We found [what is] the most successful about the model of service is coordination, maximizing benefits for the client, and avoiding duplication in a way to not overwhelm the client by repeating the stories of their traumatic experiences."

(Community service provider)

"The single most important factor in linking MRCSSI and CAS services are the personal relationships between workers at the two agencies. When the time was taken to create a personal relationship, trust became much easier, particularly considering the solutions we were seeking were at times out of everyone's comfort zone. A reasonable level of trust is critical on both sides!"

(Children's Aid Society manager)

"I think that the integration with the mosque has been important – that spiritual leaders in the community have endorsed this model has given it tremendous credibility – especially in the early work of the agency. From an agency perspective – the manner in which the links were established was very integral to the success. MRCSSI took great care to educate the community partners, weave us into their strategic planning and involve us in the service development right from the beginning."

(Community service provider)

4 Early Intervention

In this chapter, we describe the early identification and intervention stage of the violence and response continuum associated with the Culturally Integrative Family Safety Response (CIFSR) model (see Figure 4.1). These responses are aimed at identifying risk factors and intervening with families before situations escalate and require mandated service involvement. We present the CIFSR model as it operates in the early stages of supporting families in concert with broader system involvement. We discuss how the model works for supporting families when others have noticed risk factors but no reports have been made or action taken by mandated service providers such as the courts or child protection agencies. We also describe CIFSR early support and interventions for families who are already involved with mandated service providers. We identify early interventions when risk is reported but deemed to be minimal to moderate, as well as mandated interventions following a more critical incident such as an act of violence directed at another family member. This includes families working with programs or agencies prior to action on the part of child protection agencies to remove persons from the family home. In this chapter we present the principles and applications of the Four Aspects Screening Tool (FAST) and the Coordinated Organizational Response Team (CORT) for early interventions with families. The application of FAST and CORT approaches for more critical and complex family circumstances is described in Chapter 5.

What Do We Mean by "Early Intervention"?

We think about CIFSR early intervention in two ways. The first of these is when the risk or incidence of family violence is known only by people within the family or community of origin and not known by mandated services. The second form of early intervention is when risk is identified by schools or family physicians, for example, who are not providing a mandated service and where risk is low to moderate. In these latter situations, the incident may be reported to legally mandated services such as child protection or police, and CIFSR may be used to modify the response by

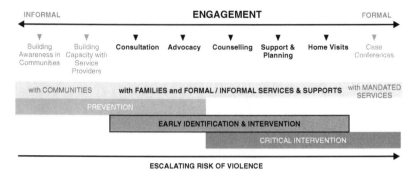

Figure 4.1 CIFSR Engagement Continuum at Early Intervention

these services while not necessarily using intrusive interventions such as removing a family member from the home.

In the first type of early intervention (see Figure 4.2), risk factors are present, others in the family or community have noticed them, and no reports have yet been made nor action taken by the courts or child protection agencies or any other mandated services. One of the challenges of such a situation is that there can be a clash of the belief systems between service providers operating within a more individualist framework and the collectivist values held within a local cultural community. It is at these points that prior dialogue and capacity-building efforts provide a firmer basis on which to appreciate and acknowledge the competing nature of these belief systems and how they can affect early interventions and supports for families at risk. For example, because of the secrecy that serves to protect family systems in a collectivist context, established service providers in the broader community are likely to be unaware of early indicators of family violence in a particular family. Sometimes, unless there is a critical incident of family violence, it is difficult to identify family members who are at risk of or already being victimized. Peers, allies, and elders are more likely to be the first line of approach for family members concerned about conflict or problems in their families. Increasing capacity and awareness for these community members means that they will have the means to respond to such concerns by providing links to appropriate resources and suggestions for next steps that will enhance family safety.

Families experiencing conflict related to parenting, couples' communication, managing the transitions associated with family migration, or responding to children and adolescents who are caught between the very different worlds of home and school, are likely to initially approach their imam or community elders for advice and guidance. Organizations involved in outreach and raising awareness about family violence may already have trusting relationships with local cultural and faith groups, and more ready

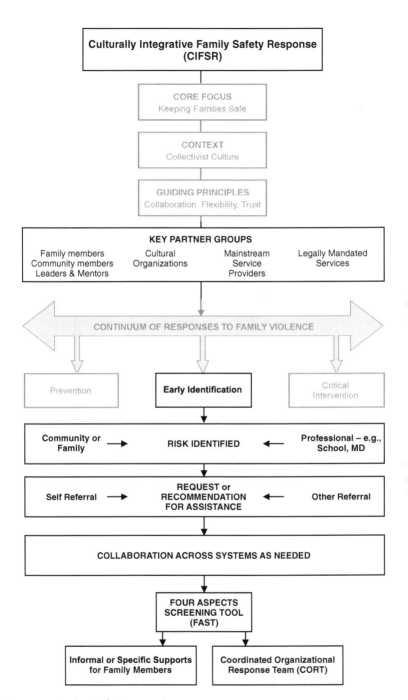

Figure 4.2 CIFSR Early Interventions

access to families on the threshold of family violence. One example of this might be where there is a risk of violence being directed toward girls and young women who are perceived as disobeying or dishonouring their family. Early awareness of such circumstances allows members of these groups or organizations to refer family members to established services in the broader community or informal supports to make early identification and interventions for safe resolution of conflict possible. Natural gathering places for families such as mosques, cultural centres, and immigrant settlement services can also be places where information about warning signs and how to seek out help and resources can provide easier access to formal and informal supports.

As described in Chapter 3, early engagement with families can also occur between family members and a wide range of service providers when family members are looking for support in solving problems identified as being related to mental health or legal concerns, or getting children to obey their parents or wives to respect their husbands. Service providers in these instances may include teachers, family physicians, settlement workers, or employment or social assistance workers. These potential "first responders" can benefit from enhanced awareness of some of the complexities and nuances of providing culturally appropriate guidance and responses beyond a relatively simple direction to the victim to "leave" and "get help." In particular, early interventions in such circumstances should include engaging the men of the family with respect and reserving judgement, while also supporting girls and women. Actively working to separate or alienate family members from one another is unlikely to be helpful in the longer term. In addition, it is valuable to be aware of and acknowledge the various pre- and post-migration stressors affecting newcomer and ethnic minority families, and the associated complexities of presenting concerns.

The second form of early intervention described previously is when risk is identified by schools, settlement services, women's shelters, family physicians, or other similar groups or individuals who are not providing mandated services, and this risk is deemed to be low or moderate. In these situations, the incident may be reported to legally mandated child protection or police services. CIFSR-guided collaborations may be used by the mandated service providers and community partners to help modify the response and perhaps avoid the most intrusive interventions of removing a family member from their home or pressing criminal charges. For example, using the assessment guidelines described later in this chapter, the Muslim Resource Centre for Social Support and Integration (MRCSSI) has been involved in discussions with the local child protection agency early in their response to a school report when they have already been working with the family. Such discussions may include whether the current risk might be considered to fall at the threshold rather than requiring direct involvement of child protection. Particularly if the current working relationship between MRCSSI and the family seems promising, the child protection agency may determine that they do not need to open a file at this time and that, for now, the best intervention is to allow ongoing support and guidance from MRCSSI.

Similarly, MRCSSI has had the experience of being involved in an early intervention with a woman who disclosed to her settlement worker that her husband had hit her several times. The settlement worker reported to the police and an arrest was made. MRCSSI started to work with the police, the settlement agency, the child protection agency, the local women's shelter, and the family to come up with a plan to prevent any escalation in intervention because the woman indicated that she simply wanted someone to tell her husband to stop the violence, but not to separate him from her and the family. This intervention entailed a response team process (see description of CORT later in this chapter) that resulted in a plan where all of the key players, including the police victim services and the women's shelter, agreed to work together. The result was that no criminal charges were brought against the husband. He agreed to continue receiving counselling from MRCSSI. The woman continued to be involved with MRCSSI and the women's shelter counselling services. At the time of this writing, the husband is working full time and has returned to live with the family; the wife is connected to her own broader social network; and both are continuing to receive counselling. The wife reports that she feels safe and that her husband has not used violence since the original concern was raised.

Four Aspects Screening Tool (FAST)

Within the CIFSR model, early identification of risk factors for family violence is intended to provide direction for interventions before situations escalate and become subject to mandated services. Through outreach to families in need or distress and in subsequent engagement with these family members, a professional service provider (for example, a mental health professional, family therapist, social worker, or psychologist with a professional level of training in screening, assessment, and psychotherapy provision) at the cultural organization or referring agency can use FAST to screen, assess, and consider appropriate referral (see Figure 4.3). FAST is used in conjunction with other standardized tools and procedures used by established service providers when assessing risk to family safety. The outcome of the FAST assessment could lead to families becoming part of a response team initiative, or family members may be engaged in individual supports and services. The FAST assessment is valuable at both the early intervention stage, as well as in preparing to work with families who are at a more critical or complex level of family violence experience. We describe FAST here (see Appendix A) and refer to it in Chapter 5 as well when referencing these more critical or complex situations.

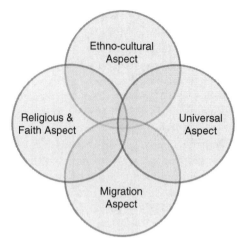

Figure 4.3 Four Aspects Screening Tool (FAST)

FAST focuses on identifying sources of risk of family violence and developing a better picture of the risks and resources within a family. The person using this tool to explore family members' relationships, family dynamics, and familial and community roles pays particular attention to understanding those dynamics that are unique to collectivist and immigrant communities, and which may be negatively contributing to family well-being and safety. These include what the FAST designates as the universal aspect (the types of stressors and relationship dynamics that can occur across cultures and groups, e.g., life cycle events or communication problems between family members); the migration aspect (pre- and post-migration experiences and stressors); the ethno-cultural aspect (gaining insight into how family members identify themselves in terms of country of origin, ethnic and cultural background, and their associated customs and traditions); and the religious and faith aspect (the role of religion in the family's life). The FAST process should guide the assessor in identifying key strengths and risks, as well as who will be the most appropriate partners for the response team. Key questions for the assessor to consider when conducting a FAST assessment are:

- What are the underlying issues?
- How have experiences, beliefs, and attitudes contributed to these issues?
- Who needs support?
- Who needs to be involved?
- Who can help?

We continue to refine the specific questions comprising the FAST guide, and our current efforts are being directed at validation. Here we describe the dimensions of the tool:

Universal Aspect

These questions invite general information about family composition, pre-senting issues, and pre-determinants of health from a collectivist immigrant perspective. They include questions about how an individual and their community of origin define family violence and how safety concerns are generally addressed in this family. The questions are designed to be appro-priate to ask to build information about the context of family violence in the family's local community. They are unique to immigrant collectivist families, exploring community perceptions and barriers in health, education, and economics. There are seven main dimensions (23 subheadings and 43 items) in the universal aspect:

- Demographics
- Family structure
- Universal nature of conflict/presenting issues
- Health
- Education
- Family economics
- Family support (providing or receiving)

Migration Aspect

Questions in this aspect elicit information about pre-migration trauma, acculturation level and type, and post-migration stressors in order to under-stand some of the pre- and post-migration challenges that family members have faced and their relative success or failure to integrate. Mental health status and access to outreach services are influenced by these factors in the lives of immigrant families affected by family violence. Questions about a family's migratory experiences require sensitivity and are posed in an open-ended manner. The migration aspect includes three main dimensions (nine subheadings and 32 items):

- Migration experience
- Witnessing experiences of war and conflict
- Post migration

Ethno-cultural Aspect

These questions allow the assessor to gain a better picture of a family's customs and traditions, and thus a clearer understanding of potential risks and resources present. The questions go beyond a simple knowledge of the origins of the family, and are designed to provide insight into the diverse ethnic and cultural backgrounds of communities and regions. For example, not all Muslims are Arabs, and not all Arabs are Muslims. The common ground within a Muslim community is the religion of Islam and not culture, ethnicity, country of origin, or language. These questions invite family members to describe how they identify themselves and their cultural references. This aspect has three main dimensions (nine subheadings and 30 items):

- Cultural dynamics
- Family dynamics
- Sense of belonging/support and safety

Religious and Faith Aspect

The questions within this aspect are used by the assessor carefully and with respect as they touch on very sensitive issues. Sometimes religion forms the basis of beliefs about family and gender relationships. For other communities, religion is less important. These questions invite family members to describe how their community defines the role played by religion in everyday life. This will likely guide the role of religion in the family's life. It is important for the assessor to honour the belief system of the family members who are being served. This aspect has four main dimensions (nine items):

- Religious/faith views
- Role/impact of religion/faith in daily life
- Role/impact of religion/faith in family
- Support/belonging to religious community

Coordinated Organizational Response Teams (CORT)

As we stated earlier, part of the FAST approach to identifying risk factors includes determining which services and support persons might be most suitable to bring together to ensure safety in the family. Sometimes, the outcome of this early assessment is to connect families to culturally appropriate individual, couple, or family therapy, or other programs that fit their current circumstances and are offered by service providers who have a strong grounding in cultural competency and safety. In many cases the FAST assessor will recommend a customized response to unique family circumstances, oriented to helping the family overcome challenges that could affect or are affecting their safety. In these instances, a CORT is established by the professional service provider who has conducted the FAST. This professional may be an employee of the cultural organization, the organization originally connected with the family, or the mandated service agency. It should be noted that, while a mandated service provider can institute and maintain the CORT process, some flexibility may be lost if a critical event or investigation requires the application of the mandated organization's policies and procedures rather than a customized response. The CORT structures a unique collaborative group of service providers and community members who are directly involved with this family. This caring collaborative group of professionals and community members forms around the family, addressing risks for family violence and supporting successful culturally integrative family safety responses. Over time, the structure of the CORT may be adapted to meet changing family needs.

The CORT is intended to ensure that services are well coordinated to avoid gaps, overlaps, or contradictory directions. This is especially important when working with newcomer families who are dealing with relocation, adaptation, and acculturation that may leave these family members confused and uncertain about service provision in their new home country. In addition, issues related to pre-migration trauma and personal and family stresses associated with significant transitions may be exacerbated by a lack of coordination or poor communication amongst service providers. Similarly, communication that takes cultural and language differences explicitly into account can be more practically managed when the team has a clear and consistent means of connecting in a culturally integrative manner across the support network and family.

The CORT, as a collaborative group of service providers and community members, together with family members, allows a greater potential to deliver a holistic approach to physical, mental, and social well-being. All of the CORT members are responsible for collaboratively developing, through transparent means, a culturally appropriate plan for keeping this family safe. While individual CORT members differ depending on the particular needs of a family, the core of each team includes the coordinating organization, family physician, referring agency, a community or religious leader, family members, and school personnel when there are children in the family.

Structure and Composition of the CORT

Typically, the organization that has developed a relationship with the family is a good choice as a coordinator. However, issues of time, resources, and agency mandate may limit their ability to take on this role and an alternative organization may be in a better position to do so. In any case, the coordinating organization takes responsibility for completing the initial screening and identification of risk factors, and then facilitating communication and actions between the various support persons and the family to ensure a culturally integrative response. Confidentiality practices include having the clients involved sign consent forms to allow the sharing of information between service providers. The skills required for this coordinating task include: planning, time management, relationship building, and group facilitation. An integration counsellor with a background in social work, psychology, family therapy, or a related field, and who understands the cultural context of the specific collectivist community where the family resides, is most often responsible for this level of coordination. In MRCSSI's experience, the integration counsellor is an employee of the cultural organization, which is also the primary coordinating organization for CIFSR partnerships in the community.

The early FAST assessment will help the coordinating organization identify the key formal stakeholders required for supporting a particular family in need. As members of the response team, the service providers' roles are twofold: to provide support to the families involved, and to work collaboratively with the other stakeholders on culturally integrative responses. Each provider's involvement may be time limited or longer term according to the unique needs of the family members. This fluidity of engagement allows for integrative services that directly address the family's needs and context at a particular point in time and over the course of the team's involvement. The integration counsellor and/or other team members from the cultural organization take on the particular responsibility of ensuring that other team members are supported in understanding the particular cultural aspects of the family members' lives and challenges. The team members all serve to respectfully share their perspectives, influenced by agency mandates and professional training, with other team members in the interest of ensuring full attention to the complex integration of factors impinging on each family member's experience and responses. An important criterion for involvement in the CORT is a willingness on the part of team members to reach beyond their respective mandates to respond to family need and risk factors in potentially unique or customized ways.

Community partners can include supports such as religious or cultural organizations, community leaders, elders, imams, and community members with specific areas of expertise. When engaged in a response team, these individuals and groups can provide unique levels of support and encouragement to the family, bringing an explicit cultural context that is often missing from more established organizational supports. The engagement of these team members allows for important knowledge sharing between the formal and informal sectors of social support in the community. Such dialogue builds the capacity within the informal sector for supporting others in the community and extending awareness of resources related to health, well-being, and safety. In addition, more formal and established organizations benefit from learning more about the context of newcomer families, the lived experience of migration and pre-migration trauma, and resources within the religious and cultural communities.

Similar to CIFSR-guided inclusion of community partners, the involvement of family members within the CIFSR model is a key to maintaining focus on the collectivist context for the families who are being supported by these interventions. This involvement can occur in at least two ways according to the model – involving the family members who are at risk, and involving other family members who will support family safety. Often it is one family member who approaches or comes to the attention of a service-providing agency – a woman who is feeling unsafe in her home, children who may be at risk, parents and teens who are in conflict, couples who are having difficulty in their relationships, adults or young people who are in trouble with the police. It is important early on to determine who else in the family should be included as support for the response team. The integration counsellor, as part of assessing the situation at home and in the family, will make recommendations for who to involve based on their potential to serve as supportive mentors. These recommendations may include elders or others who can provide a cultural context for decision making and family problem solving, sounding boards for parents, and trusted voices in young persons' lives. The involvement of others will ensure that there is enough support from within the family for those who are at risk or victims of violence. It is best to include at least one family member who will be very supportive and encourage the victim to ask for outside help.

The first step in making this selection is to ask the family member who has come forward and is currently at risk about her (or his) perspectives and feelings about who in the family should be involved. In the case of intimate partner violence, for example, the woman who is at risk or has been harmed will have some experience about how key members from her family and her spouse's family are likely to respond. She will be knowledgeable about who is likely to be more understanding of the potential risks, and to support changes contributing to more safety for all family members. The integration counsellor will listen to the client's statements and assessment, and also engage in some form of family mapping (how big the family is and who the key members are, both here and back home; how decisions are usually made about issues significant to the family; blood relationships between the couples; and socioeconomic status of both spouses). In many cases, there are some members from the perpetrator's relatives who could be more supportive than someone from the victim's family. These are assessments and decisions that the integration counsellor would do at the very beginning of his or her involvement. Here we are talking about cases of early intervention where sometimes mandated services are not yet involved or perhaps involved only at very early stages.

The FAST assessment guides the identification of family members whose voices should be heard during CORT deliberations. The members of CORT determine whether it is best to have family members directly involved in attending meetings, or to more indirectly ensure their voices are represented by someone else (for example, the integration counsellor from the culturally based organization who works most closely with the family). Indirect contributions require that the integration counsellor, for example, meet with family members prior to a CORT meeting and incorporate their voices into the report to CORT, and then that she/he represents these perspectives during the CORT meeting.

Over the course of the family's involvement with the CIFSR team, the team will consider how current supports are working and how various family members are responding to these. Such considerations may lead to more or less involvement with some of the family members based on the level of risk in the family and the understanding these persons have about the seriousness of the risk. Their continued involvement also depends on how they perceive the implications for family unity of the ongoing involvement of mandated services. In our experience at MRCSSI we try to show these family members how cooperation with the service providers at an early stage could reduce any negative consequences for the unity of the family.

We have heard many families state their concern that the family could break down if the perpetrator were to be arrested or the children are removed from the family and placed with a family of strangers. Educating family members about how the system works and that the state doesn't necessarily have an interest in breaking down families or taking children away from their families provides a very good starting point for establishing meaningful communication and building trust between them and the response team. A very good example of this kind of situation is when a child protection worker is involved with a family because of a report of child abuse. Our role as a bridge in this instance focuses on helping both the family and the child protection agency to not escalate the conflict and the misunderstanding. The family can be encouraged to cooperate with the child protection worker and agree voluntarily to place the child with an extended family member or a kinship family until the investigation is completed. In return, the child protection agency would not proceed with asking for a court order to remove the child from their home, while still having more say in determining when it is safe for the child to return home. In such instances, we have seen very positive outcomes, where the child eventually returns home and the family takes responsibility for their abusive actions, agreeing to attend counselling with our organization while continuing to work with the child protection agency to implement their child-centred plan of service.

At MRCSSI we have also been involved in situations where the family's loyalty appears to be divided between a woman who has come forward with concerns about her safety and her husband. When we have been able to assess the extended family's relationship dynamics and identify those who are and are not supportive of the wife, we have subsequently been able to strengthen the position of those who showed more empathy toward her. This has allowed the response team to later work with those who were not originally supportive of a family member at risk of being harmed. It is important to note that the family's involvement in the CIFSR model of service provision is always voluntary (i.e., they can engage in more traditional programs or established supports in the broader community without the team involvement if they wish) – their ongoing consent is central to this model of care.

In order for the partner groups working together to provide services to families within the CIFSR model, and individual team members who become part of the collaborative response team working with a particular family, to work effectively and respectfully with each other and the family, clear communication strategies are very important. At the heart of this type of service is client consent and engagement in the process. Family members, from the moment that they contact a service provider and continuing through assessment, the establishment of a coordinated organizational response team, and the course of time during which they are engaged in working together with the team, must consent to their own involvement and have options to withdraw and engage in different types of services that may also be available to them. Issues of confidentiality, exposure within a smaller community, and involvement with a number of persons and organizations simultaneously may be factors in the comfort that family members experience as part of this provision of support. It is critical to listen to and acknowledge these expressed concerns, and to be willing to talk about alternatives, misperceptions, and potentially unrealistic expectations. These early discussions, as well as issues that arise over time, should be addressed by the integration counsellor and coordinating organization. It is the coordinating organization's responsibility to ensure that the family members are freely providing informed consent to participate and to continue participation over time.

Similarly, response team members should engage in discussions with each other, early and often, about the limits of their time and resources, and about their expectations with regard to outcome and process. If memoranda of understanding or partnership agreements are in place between organizations, these should be reviewed by the team members at the initiation of their work together. Similarly, a group-determined process of communication ensures collaboration is not hindered by lack of information or by misunderstandings. This could include, for example, consideration of the means of communication, notice and scheduling of face-to-face meetings, how and when to make contact between team members and the coordinator, and notification of when work of the response team has been completed or work with the family discontinued. Discussion of communication processes, and ongoing attention to these, includes close attention to how decisions are being made and communicated to family members at the heart of the response team's work. The coordinator will be responsible for encouraging and ensuring respectful communication between various sectors, and between team members who work within a more formal professional or organizational context and those who represent more informal or community supports. The potential for misunderstanding based on language is significant, so resources should be directed to providing translation services as needed. In addition, the "languages" used by certain professional groups and service sectors may be quite unintelligible to others who do not regularly work within these organizational contexts, and these differences as well should be taken into account.

Intervention planning begins with case conferencing by CORT members (the victim may be present, and family members' voices would be represented at this early stage by the worker most familiar with the family and community – usually from the cultural organization). Collaborative dialogue about the FAST outcome summary allows all team members to come together to discuss a plan for meeting the needs of the family. In addition, CORT members can discuss some of the challenges, struggles, and solutions that they are considering or facing in responding to the family's unique circumstances. The plan of action directs the CORT in shaping itself around the family's needs. The team members also support each other in delivering services and supports beyond the scope of each member organization's mandate by entering "shadow zones" that fall outside of their traditional policies and procedures. Stretching the boundaries of their service provision allows organizations and groups to provide better supports to keep the family safe. CORT members are also able to develop reciprocal relationships that allow them to educate one another about the cultural context of the family, structural aspects of service-providing and mandated organizations, and specific safety issues that need to be addressed. During this planning and early implementation of the plan, it is likely that further family strengths and risk factors will be identified and these can be taken into account in ongoing planning.

The CORT participants prepare an informal document that outlines the roles, responsibilities, and expectations of all team members. Family members' voices are sought directly or indirectly (through the cultural organization's worker, for example) to contribute to this document, depending on the CORT determination. This document provides structure for the implementation of the plan that follows. Typically, the CORT meets every three months to review the family's circumstances and safety, the relative effectiveness of the combined efforts of the service providers and support network, and any changing needs that have become evident over time. This process of implementation and review by CORT will continue for up to a year or longer, depending on the needs of the family. This active collaboration and idea sharing is integral to intervening prior to escalation of risk factors in the family. The CORT engages in a cyclical process of identifying and addressing ongoing and emergent risks associated with family violence, as well as family adaptiveness in terms of newly evident resourcefulness and connections with the local community. CORT members monitor changes for family members and the family system, and adaptations to the constellation of service providers and support persons, as well as which family members are engaged, are implemented by the team as necessary.

Each CORT's structure, plan, and implementation strategy will be different. This is to be expected in response to the unique characteristics and circumstances of each family. Ensuring that cultural aspects of family life, risk factors, strengths, and the role of the local community are integrated into all service provision is a key element of the CORT's successful implementation of the plan. It is also important that team members recognize that there are likely to be vast differences between the solutions envisaged by organizations within the broader community relying primarily on established practices, and those considered by community members following cultural traditions or collectivist principles. Culturally integrated interventions will require partners from established service-providing organizations to think differently about the role of the local collectivist community. The CORT allows partners to incorporate the moral, religious, or cultural authority of community partners into established interventions, all oriented to keeping families safe. The following questions are helpful in guiding the CORT collaborations:

- What are we (CORT partners) worried about?
- What is working well?
- Is there any missing information?
- What needs to happen?
- What are the agency/family/community goals?
- What will agencies need to see occurring in order for them to be willing to close the case?
- What does the family want generally and regarding safety?
- What are the next steps?
- What would indicate to agencies that some progress has been made?

Case Example: FAST and CORT in Action (Said)

The following case example is based on actual client work, with details and descriptions altered so as not to identify actual persons. The descriptions and reflections in this example were provided by members of the MRCSSI clinical team: Eugene Tremblay and Mohammed Baobaid.

Initial Involvement

Said's father initially contacted MRCSSI requesting help because he was concerned about the relationship between his 9-year-old son, Said, and his wife. He stated also that his son was physically aggressive, and his own preference to engage the services of a Muslim organization. The family did not engage immediately, but when school personnel became aware of the father's request, they contacted MRCSSI to provide help and support. At that time, school personnel were concerned about Said's relationship with his peers, in particular his aggressiveness in the school and community. They were also concerned that the child appeared delayed intellectually and that it had been very difficult for them to engage the family. At this point, MRCSSI counsellors again contacted the family and they readily engaged, focusing on Said's struggles at school and in the community. Over the next six months MRCSSI involved a children's mental health organization to provide services to the family and child, and this organization recommended that Said's needs would be best met through a short-term residential placement. This recommendation was explored at a case conference between MRCSSI and the children's mental health organization. Given the family's unwillingness to consider such a placement, the children's mental health organization proceeded with a family preservation intervention. MRCSSI staff attended scheduled sessions with the family to support their engagement with this children's mental health intervention, and the family, including Said, also attended sessions to encourage adaptive parenting and helping Said manage his behaviours. After a year of involvement with the family on the part of the school, MRCSSI, and children's mental health agency, the group decided to involve child protection services. There had been, in the previous eight months, three separate reports and investigations by the child protection service agency. At this point, MRCSSI had been involved with the family for at least 18 months, facilitating family engagement in supportive services; bringing in a Muslim paediatrician from outside the city who spoke the language of the family to explain to the family the need for specialized resources for the children to meet their needs; and involving two local imams to help the family understand their obligations to the children under Islam. The child protection agency, given that this was their plan of service, became the lead for interventions with this family. In collaboration with MRCSSI, they initiated the CORT and jointly invited other groups such as the mosque, the school, and the settlement agency. In follow up, MRCSSI coordinated the community support that was part of the overall plan developed by the CORT.

Presenting Concerns

Said was presenting difficulties in the household, school, and community, and these were concerning for other family members and school personnel, and threatened his own safety. He had been involved in bullying, shoplifting, hitting his mother with a steel bar, smashing the sides of the family car, and smashing the home computer when he was upset. Said was not regularly attending school and he had been involved with the police on different occasions due to his violent behaviour. Said had a long history of being bullied in a previous community and school he attended. He was often engaged by peers to threaten others and his role became defined within peer groups as the "heavy."

A couple of years earlier, Said had been admitted to the hospital after disclosing that he heard voices instructing him to kill someone. While not connecting these previous concerns to what they were observing now, Said's parents identified their worries about his mental health based on these behaviours: he did not like to eat with his siblings at the dinner table and only engaged with them if he needed something; he had been suspended from school many times due to his bullying behaviours; and he was often scared to sleep without the lights on in his bedroom. The family identified as being highly religious, seeking online religious knowledge (Qu'ran lessons) in their own language. When Said broke the computer, it produced a crisis within the family.

Interventions and Support

The FAST conducted by MRCSSI highlighted the important role of religion for this family and identified potential benefits to moving closer to the mosque. The family arranged to make this move and notified MRCSSI when the move was completed. They engaged in traditional cultural practices reflecting their ethno-cultural community. The parents did not accept a special education program for their special needs children, stating that the children "should get more help from school" without placing them into the special program. The universal factors of mental health, poverty, and intergenerational conflict were also identified using FAST.

When a CORT was convened, the following organizations were involved (the family appointed a family friend with a shared cultural background to represent them in this instance):

- Child protection agency – To work along with MRCSSI in supporting this family and increasing the parents' capacity to parent.
- MRCSSI (cultural broker) – To become the main source of support helping the family navigate through all other services involved and provide a cultural and religious framework for interventions that were offered.
- School – To work along with all the other services in order to increase Said's capacity to learn.
- Children's mental health agency – To provide group therapy for Said related to behaviour management.
- Children's mental health services organization – To provide residential treatment for Said's safety and well-being.
- Local mosque – To provide religious support, enhance the well-being of all family members, and invite increased community connection and support for the family.
- Police victim support services – To provide link to police given their involvement.

The CORT supported the following actions aimed at building more supports for this family in the community:

- Mentorship for the boys in the family – a trained mentor was provided by MRCSSI with the mosque providing funding for this initially.
- School agreed to address Said's learning difficulties in the special education classroom. The family agreed to accept this because of the involvement of their family friend in the decision-making process. However, they considered this to be somewhat problematic.
- At the early stage of intervention, the child protection agency was in the process of arranging residential treatment for Said through the children's mental health agency. Through careful consideration at the CORT level, and ongoing consideration of what was best for him and his family, the CORT changed the plan to one that kept him in his family home and provided for more community support for the family.
- To address a primary concern of the child protection agency, which was the parents' capacity to deal with their children and family stressors,

informal supports were identified and put in place. These included a support person who was a member of their cultural community, as well as faith community support through the mosque.

- Continued involvement with the family allowed the CORT group to see that the other children in the family also had concerns and challenges. These challenges included the older sibling who seemed to present a more isolated nature and also functioned with intellectual delays. Since these behaviours were more internalized, this sibling appeared to be neglected and promoted by the school system. The younger sibling was seen unsupervised in the community at the beginning of our involvement around areas that may have presented a risk to the child's safety. In addition, this sibling presented more significant delays alongside a more pleasant and engaging manner. These needs were then incorporated into the overall plan for the family.

- A voluntary service agreement, with clear expectations of parents as well as partner agencies, was developed by MRCSSI and the child protection agency. The participants in the CORT identified what needed to be in place in order to keep Said with his family. These requirements included responsibilities for each of the agency partners' involvement with the CORT, as well as MRCSSI's agreement to facilitate and coordinate support from the community. The parents signed an agreement as part of the requirement to keep Said at home. This parental agreement included looking for professional help related to parenting and coping with various stressors.

Impact and Outcomes

- The primary supports in place for this family included the cultural organization (MRCSSI), the child protection agency, and the mosque. Said was reported to be doing better at school due to support provided by the principal, educational assistant, and teacher.

- The mosque had focused on Said's self-esteem by providing mentorship opportunities, community connections, and a volunteer job for Said as a security guard. In addition, they provided Qu'ran lessons during Ramadan and another month, and, free of charge, summer camp.

- For the family, the mosque had provided religious support. Since he was seen by the family as an important resource and figure, the imam acted to minimize the family's guilt and shame at one point by normalizing the difficulties they were going through.

Reflections from Mohammed

I see this as a typical example of a complex case that included clear indication of potential high risk for family violence. It is common in this kind of situation, using traditional interventions, that the case would be assessed as high risk by mandated services, including child protection services and the police, and that they would be more intrusive in their intervention. It would be most likely that Said would spend some time in a residential treatment centre, and that he would continue to struggle with his family as well as at school. After age 12, he would be charged for offences with police involvement. The family would likely continue to blame the school system for not helping their child, in particular for creating obstacles to ongoing schooling and his success in the future. The child protection agency would most likely extend their concerns to the other children in the family, and potentially remove them from their family home as well. In such circumstances, Said could have some more difficulties that contribute to an identity crisis that might lead him to join gangs or extreme groups in order to seek a sense of belonging.

At MRCSSI we believe that the use of FAST helped us to recognize risk sources as early as possible and accordingly develop a more culturally adapted response and support. We also see that the CORT process was very helpful with respect to identifying all of the key groups and individuals who needed to be at the table and focusing the conversation based on the result of FAST assessment. This provided a context in which to develop a sound plan for service that was culturally sound and effective. While this alternative intervention takes a lot of time, we see this outcome as amazing and proactive with regard to potential longer-term risks and outcomes.

What community service providers have to say...

"Another helpful aspect was the MRCSSI's ability to delve into the detailed personal and social circumstances of the clients and families, given the extra time they had (compared to my limited time as a family doctor) and their linguistic and cultural competency. This provided far greater insight into clients' circumstances and into other issues (for example, school attendance) that would not have otherwise been known to me."

(Physician – CORT participant)

"Many families we worked with had complex needs requiring extensive collaboration amongst service providers. The team at MRCSSI was small in comparison to many organizations yet always willing to be present to do this challenging work. My experience with many families we mutually served has been one of transformation in large part because of the support, collaboration and interventions of MRCSSI. As an organization, MRCSSI has made important links with many service providers in the community and established many collaborations that have resulted in changes to how Muslim families receive and engage with services in our community."

(Community service provider)

5 Engaging with Complex, High-risk Situations and Broader Systems

As described earlier, interventions grounded in the Culturally Integrative Family Safety Response (CIFSR) model are made along a continuum (see Figure 5.1). These range from preventative responses (see Chapter 2), to early identification and intervention (see Chapter 3), to more complex and high-risk interventions that involve mandated services and perhaps several different agencies. In this chapter, we discuss supports and interventions related to these latter, higher-risk situations. These more critical and complex interventions (see Figure 5.2) utilize the same tools, organizational context, and CIFSR approach described to this point (i.e., Coordinated Organizational Response Team [CORT] and Four Aspects Screening Tool [FAST]). However, due to potentially greater risk for families, these circumstances demand careful and ongoing attention to assessing and addressing the safety of potential victims, and coordinating the roles of multiple service-providing organizations and support persons. Most often, in these cases, leadership for the overall intervention is provided by the mandated service provider rather than the cultural organization/broker. In these situations, the police or court systems and the child protection system are already involved in addressing family violence and safety concerns in the family. When a mandated response is required, there may be less flexibility initially in customizing a response and the case conference managed by the mandated organization will be guided primarily by their typical protocols and procedures. However, this does not preclude a CORT being formed to function in a more advisory capacity, particularly over time, to ensure a culturally integrative response in the longer term. The role of the cultural organization/broker is different here than it may be with preventative and earlier responses and interventions. The immediacy, risk, and complexity of these situations require attention to priorities and risk, as well as relevant mandates for safety and protection.

Contributing to High-risk Case Conferences

As stated earlier, critical interventions that involve mandated services are led by the mandated service. Thus, high-risk case conferences will follow the existing protocols in these organizations for these types of interventions – for

Culturally Integrative Family Safety Response Engagement Continuum

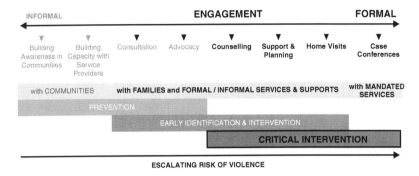

Figure 5.1 CIFSR Engagement Continuum at Critical Interventions

example, in cases of child abuse or intimate partner violence. Cultural organizations like the Muslim Resource Centre for Social Support and Integration (MRCSSI) will play a more consultative role to both service providers and family members as part of the high-risk case conference. In many ways, interventions guided by CIFSR will not differ from any high-risk case conferences in cases of child abuse or intimate partner violence. Due to the high-risk designation and leadership from the mandated agency, the focus will initially be primarily on immediate risk reduction with little room to consider existing strengths within the family. It is MRCSSI's experience that the outcome in these kinds of situations, when guided by existing protocols, is to ensure safety of the victim by forcing the perpetrator to not associate directly or indirectly with the victim, often involving removal of one or more family members from the home. In many cases where I (Mohammed) have been involved, my role has been to help the family, and also the child protection agency, women's shelter workers, and police to restore the trust that is usually disrupted when such intrusive interventions are made by the mandated agency.

One important strategy in these cases is to encourage service providers to recognize strength elements within the family or within the community and consider them in their intervention process. These strengths may be aspects of family life and individual family members' contributions that MRCSSI is more familiar with due to earlier meetings and/or FAST assessments with the family. Our associations in the collectivist community during prevention or awareness-building activities may also have provided us with additional knowledge of these family members or their extended network.

Second, at MRCSSI we work to invite the case conference participants and service providers working with the family following the initial intervention to consider a move away from viewing family members solely in terms of perpetrators or victims of violence. The direct and indirect influences of participation in and exposure to violence at the level of social, political,

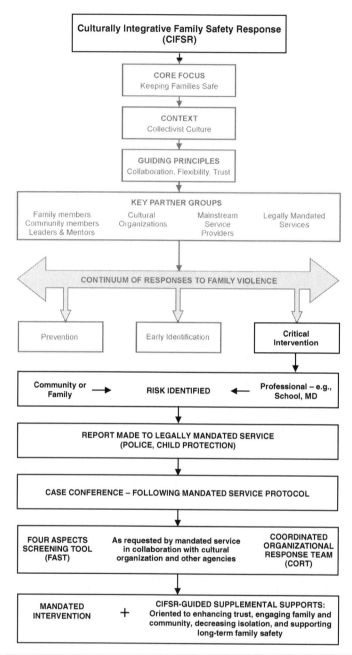

Figure 5.2 CIFSR Critical Interventions for Complex, High-risk Situations

and personal interactions are much more complex for collectivist families coming from conflict zones than this simple dichotomy of perpetrator/victim suggests. It is important for mandated services involved in maintaining safety for family members to be aware of the unique journey and context of each family. As a collective entity, families within these communities are rooted in complex social, political, and tribal contexts. In many cases the whole family considers themselves survivors of war, conflict, and trauma at multiple levels.

In the families with whom MRCSSI has been involved, it is usually the case that the man in the family has been directly victimized by war, imprisonment, or torture. This man will have been seen, by himself and other family members, as the protector of the whole family and the one who would sacrifice his life in order to rescue his family and manage escape from the conflict and war zone. In such a case, once the family has settled into the host community, a report of family violence on the part of this man will place the victim of this violence in the very difficult position of making a complaint against a husband, father, or son who has also been a victim of different forms of violence and has acted to move the family to a safer home. These loyalty dilemmas and conflicting ties will likely lead to family members continuing to have contact with each other, despite non-association orders. Couples may meet secretly on their own or with trusted family or community members serving as informal mediators. Children may run away from their foster homes to return to families of origin, or leave school at lunchtime to see family members when a no-contact order is in place.

Carefully considered interventions need to include assistance for all family members to stop the violence and maintain safety in the event of such contact. Service providers can propose more effective interventions when they are able to take into account who in the family or community, here or back home, will be seen as potentially supportive of resolving current problems or conflict. Then, those supports for family safety can be mobilized in synchrony with formal supports rather than potentially serving to undermine or keep secret other measures for maintaining family connections.

At the formal level of service provision, the cultural organization can advocate for, and perhaps provide, counselling or therapy services alongside more intrusive removal of family members from the home. Such formalized services that augment the initial intervention to maintain safety can be, for example, directed at addressing the complex constellation of factors such as history of various types of trauma and violence for family members seen as both perpetrators and victims.

The involvement of a cultural organization such as MRCSSI serves to mediate or support trust-building between family members and mandated service providers, and this is very helpful in high-risk and complex situations. Through supportive counselling and specialized trauma therapy similar to what we offer through MRCSSI, perpetrators of violence can be invited to see and understand the new context in which they are living and the potential benefits of cooperating with the mandated services. In the case of involvement by child protection services, for example, a father could be encouraged to voluntarily agree for his child to be removed, perhaps to a kinship home from the same community or another foster family, until the current family situation has been worked out and the risk reduced. Our involvement in engaging the father in this way can facilitate communication and support trust building, allowing the child protection service to agree to not escalate the intervention prematurely by taking the case to court, for example. Similarly, in the case of spousal violence, a husband may be encouraged by a counsellor at our agency to take responsibility for his actions and attend counselling directed at ensuring safe and non-violent interactions at home alongside understanding the impact of his own history of experiences that contribute to his use of violence. With such counselling in place, the involved parties, including the probation office, may be able to come up with a less potentially isolating plan that includes supervised access to his children, possibilities for couple or family counselling, and potentially lifting the non-association order.

Even in the case of critical interventions with high-risk situations, there are benefits to the involvement of cultural organizations that have built relationships with service providers and community members. These organizations can provide supports and services to family members in addition to and alongside more intrusive interventions that maintain safety in the immediate short term. They can also facilitate tension reduction between mandated services and the family in the face of these interventions, and restore trust on both sides. It is, of course, up to the mandated service whether they will choose to use a differential response that incorporates CIFSR principles or follow business as usual. These decisions will likely be made by mandated service providers with particular regard to what makes them feel most comfortable and in control of risk factors. If there is a worker who is willing to try something different, or a historical relationship and positive track record at the agency level, then there may be opportunities to enhance the recognition of cultural context and collectivist influences with ongoing adaptation of interventions. In these situations, a cultural organization such as MRCSSI can play a critical role in helping both parties restore trust and communicate in a respectful way.

When engaging with all parties, the cultural organization can also encourage involvement of family and extended family members. In the event that a couple or family decide to circumvent the attempts of mandated services to impose conditions for safety and instead seek the informal support of trusted third parties such as tribes or extended family back home, safety may be extremely compromised. If, on the other hand, trusted family and community members can be brought in early on, they may become key supporters of measures taken to ensure long-term and ongoing safety for the family.

In summary, CIFSR-informed support can augment legally mandated interventions with collectivist families who are at high risk for family violence. While not directing the protocol of high-risk case conferences, the cultural organization can play an important role in the following ways:

- Participate in case conferences, providing information about the specific ethno-cultural aspects of the collectivist community and/or this particular family's journey and context, as well as drawing attention to family strengths.
- Following interventions, particularly those that remove family members from their homes, facilitate trust building and communication between family members and mandated service providers.
- Provide ancillary services that will support long-term family safety, such as counselling directed at identifying and managing the impact of previous exposure to social and political violence.
- Advocate for measures that will reduce isolation and secrecy. These might include promoting supervised access to children, for example, or explicitly involving, from early on, those family or community members who the family sees as mentors or supporters and who the cultural organization knows will be most likely to support safety and non-violence. Similarly, it is important to identify and mitigate the risk of negative involvement from non-supportive family or community members.
- Where the mandated service is willing, encourage the development of an advisory CORT that can serve to monitor the impact of various interventions and consult with the mandated service in addressing other aspects of family members' needs or changing family context.

CIFSR-informed Interventions Related to High-risk and Complex Family Circumstances: Two Examples

The following case examples are based on actual client work, with details and descriptions altered so as to not identify actual persons. The descriptions and reflections on these examples were provided by members of the MRCSSI clinical team – Sahar Atalla, Abir al Jamal, and Mohammed Baobaid.

Case Example I: Timeline of Early Steps in Intervention (Munir and Zina)

At the time of the events described herein, Munir was a 35-year-old Middle Eastern man married to Zina (30) with whom he had two children, an 11-year-old son and an 8-year-old daughter. Munir was unemployed, and the family's source of income was government-provided social assistance. The family had lived in Canada for less than two years. Munir was referred to MRCSSI by a local community organization providing settlement support to newcomers.

Munir had assaulted Zina in the street. He moved out of the house in an attempt to de-escalate the conflict. After a few days, Zina contacted a local women's shelter where she stayed for almost two weeks with her children.

Later on, Zina called Munir and told him that she regretted leaving the house and that she was willing to work to improve their marriage. Munir went to the police to inquire about any charges against him. There he was arrested and kept in detention overnight. He was then released with an order to have no contact with Zina or their children. Munir had access to legal aid services through MRCSSI services. When the case was filed in court, Munir was going to be represented by a lawyer provided by legal aid. However, the court hearing was postponed at that time.

Zina returned home with her children after Munir moved in with one of his relatives. She contacted MRCSSI where intake and a FAST assessment were completed.

FAST Assessment

We provide here some highlights based on the FAST notes of the MRCSSI community support worker about this couple during intake and initial assessment (the notes have been modified so as not to identify the family and do not incorporate the full assessment).

UNIVERSAL ASPECT

Munir disclosed that he was raised in an environment where he witnessed his mother being abused by his father. According to Munir, his father was an alcoholic and a gambler. Unexpectedly, Munir reported that he neither felt sorry for his mother nor was disrespectful to his father. He described his childhood as unhappy and said that he did not have any friends until he was an adolescent, when he met his only friend. He said that this friendship was very valuable and that he still maintained contact with this friend. He indicated that he had six siblings, and that he was not close to any of them. He also stated that most of his siblings had experienced marital problems. He said that his father was killed when Munir was younger, and that he accordingly left school to work at that time in order to support his family. Munir said he regretted his recent abusive behaviour and that he was committed to changing in order to get his family back and work on their marriage.

Zina reported that she was abused by Munir on several occasions. She disclosed that Munir had made decisions on her behalf and when she tried to discuss issues with him, he dismissed the subject. Zina described herself as a very organized and committed person, and her husband as a carefree person, suggesting that this caused stress in their relationship. She expressed that she wanted the abuse to stop and to keep her marriage. During the interview, Zina positioned herself in a hunched manner and her eyes reflected her sadness. She expressed that she did not have social support, but that she frequently connected via online video calls with her sister, who she described as her best friend. Zina indicated that listening to music helped her cope, as did writing when she felt overwhelmed.

MIGRATION ASPECT

The couple suffered traumatic pre-migration experiences including religious persecution, Munir's abduction, witnessing violence, and loss of a family member. Munir had a college education and the family had a good socio-economic status before migration. They experienced a downward shift in their socioeconomic status upon fleeing their home country. The family lived in financial hardship in the transit country, where Munir worked as a seller on a cart in the market to secure the basic needs of his family. Munir was Zina's protector in their country of origin and accompanied her most of the time there for security reasons. She revealed that he was also her support during her illness in the transit country. Zina attributed Munir's violent behaviour to their living circumstances after fleeing their country of origin. It was noted that, during their life in their country of origin, there was one incident of family dispute and Zina's family got involved at that time to resolve the issue. Few domestic violence incidents were exhibited in the transit country; however, these intensified in frequency in Canada. In Canada, Munir expressed worries about the future and his inability to find a job to support his family due to the language barrier. Zina attributed Munir's violent behaviour to the unstable financial circumstances they were living in and Munir's stress of being unemployed. Also, Munir stated that he was worried that Zina was changing and he would lose her as she became more assertive rather than the dependent woman he had known.

The pre-migration experiences where the family had witnessed war atrocities, and the various life challenges they faced in the transit country before they arrived in Canada, had impacted their settlement process. Post-migration stressors such as the language barrier and unemployment had added more burden to the family's lived experience. The pre- and post-migration stressors combined had a negative impact on the family dynamics so that Munir perceived himself as unable to fulfill his role as the family provider, protector, and supporter. The family's traumatic experiences that were not addressed in their early time in Canada had hindered the family's ability to move on and adjust to their new environment, and this contributed to risk of domestic violence.

ETHNO-CULTURAL ASPECT

Both Munir and Zina were originally from an Arab country but belonged to a minority ethnic group. This minority group was very patriarchal and very protective of their ethnicity and their religion. Men played a very important and protective role in their community, supported by members of the community. This created more difficulties for women who had experienced abuse and were asking for help. In their current Canadian context, the ethnic community was well connected in the province, but there were few families locally, so the family placed priority on attending community events in a large urban centre approximately two hours away. Traditionally the elders of this community would be asked to intervene in situations of family conflicts. This was very important information to identify through FAST – otherwise the family would have been considered to be like any other local Arab family, and this would be inaccurate.

RELIGIOUS AND FAITH ASPECT

Religion was central to the lives of both spouses. Their minority religious group had survived ongoing religious oppression in their country of origin, a majority Muslim country. In Canada, their religious leaders were not in their local community and, when support was required, had to be contacted in a large urban centre some two hours away. As much as Zina wanted help to stop the violence of her husband toward her, she equally did not want to be seen as someone who did not care about the collective interest of her family and community.

Outcomes

Following the FAST assessment, Zina was referred to the MRCSSI social worker. The social worker met with Zina for ten counselling sessions funded by police victim services through MRCSSI. Munir attended sessions at a Partner Assault Response (PAR) program through a local agency providing education and support services for men aimed at eliminating violent and abusive behaviour in their primary and intimate relationships. After what was deemed to be successful engagement in these different services by Zina and Munir, they received couple counselling at MRCSSI. Munir and Zina expressed that they still had feelings for each other and were committed to working on their marriage to live together as one family.

Munir indicated that he was aware that he had anger issues and had acted violently toward Zina. He stated that he was committed to changing his behaviour and to taking necessary measures in order to change, which in turn will lead him to being reunited with his family.

Munir has been assessed by a psychiatrist from the MRCSSI consultation team and he is currently taking prescribed medication. Munir attended counselling and received ongoing support from MRCSSI throughout the recent family crisis. MRCSSI has supported Munir by initiating a collaborative multi-organizational intervention where various organizations such as the probation office, court system, legal aid, child protection services, mental health services, and PAR program have come together and stretched their service delivery to meet the needs of this family.

Reflections from Mohammed

I see that this case example reflects the value of CIFSR and utilizing FAST. Working with Zina and Munir utilizing FAST gave the social worker an in-depth perspective of their lived experiences within the family context and their unique migration journey. In this case, the mandated organizations (police, court, women's shelter, child protection services, PAR program) and MRCSSI collaborated to secure family safety, supported Zina and her children, and supported Munir in being accountable for his actions by giving him the opportunity to address his anger issues and take the necessary measures to change his abusive behaviour. Looking into the family history, Munir has been subjected to abduction, and the family was persecuted. Munir is the family protector and provider. When domestic violence occurred, Zina sought help in order to stop the abuse, but she did not expect that Munir would be restrained from contact with his family, and this created a dilemma for the whole family unit. By incorporating aspects of CIFSR to support the mandated service providers in responding to risk factors, while at the same time working to ensure that the family felt heard and not negated throughout the intervention, MRCSSI was able to facilitate a more positive intervention directed at longer-term safety.

As you can see, this is a complex case that involves pre- and post-migration stressors and significant cultural differences between the cultural tradition of the family and their new Canadian context. There are a few things that I would like to highlight in regards to this case. Both Munir and Zina come from a minority group in their country of origin with only a very few people from their cultural and faith community in Canada. Thus, they are very much attached to each other and anxious about breaking their relationship. Zina decided early on in her stay at the women's shelter to go back to her husband to reconcile with him. She thought that she would be simply able to tell the shelter workers and the police that this was her wish, and that she could have her husband come back to the family. She was surprised that he was not allowed to communicate with her and their children directly or indirectly. What is really interesting in this case is that the women's shelter, police victim services, and the immigrant settlement organization were all familiar with the CIFSR model and the work of MRCSSI in general based on past collaborations. This familiarity allowed for very helpful collaboration. The women's shelter worker not only acted as an advocate for Zina, but also, based on understanding her dilemma and working within the CIFSR model, was able to encourage other mandated services to make the necessary accommodations to support Zina's goal to integrate her husband into their family without compromising her safety and the safety of her children. The whole process of engagement was an educational opportunity for all of the parties involved in this case. Service providers had opportunities to learn more about the cultural context of the family and, most importantly, to develop a balanced intervention that considered cultural context without compromising the safety of women and children victimized by family violence. Zina was able to experience real help from her own perspective, and felt empowered and supported and not rushed to one solution only. Munir also had an opportunity to learn that what happened to him was not because of his wife's actions, but because of his choices to act violently and the associated legal consequences. He could see some hope to reconcile with his family and, in particular, with his children. It was very rewarding to see such a positive outcome in a relatively short period of time with less damage and cost than in less coordinated situations with other similar cases. It is not unusual in this kind of situation for the conflict between the partners to escalate with a significant negative impact on the woman and the children. In these situations, it is most likely that the conflict between the family and the legally mandated service providers escalates. Such escalation in risk and conflict usually leads to more intrusive and costlier interventions.

Case Example II: Influences of Pre-migration Trauma and Cultural Differences (Khalid's Family)

The family described in this case example was a refugee family who was supported by a sponsoring group sharing costs and responsibilities with the federal government. In Canada, a sponsoring group in this context is a local organization (this could be a group of families, a church, a university, or a service organization, for example) and members of this group serve to voluntarily provide a range of supports to the family. We also refer below to a "community member" who made the initial referral – in this case a member of the local Muslim community, not a member of the sponsoring group, referred the family to MRCSSI. Again, identifying details have been removed or changed to protect the confidentiality of this family.

At the time of the events described herein, Khalid was a 52-year-old father of a family consisting of himself, his wife (Suaad), and their six children. The family was sponsored by a rural community some distance outside of London. They came from a conflict zone country and lived in a refugee camp for two and half years. Prior to leaving their country of origin, Khalid was abducted and tortured for two months, his brother was killed, and he witnessed the death of his eldest son. The whole family was newly arrived in Canada, had very limited command of English and there had been interrupted school attendance for the children. The family was referred to MRCSSI by a community member when the father was seen exhibiting controlling behaviour over the mother and children. Suaad had described, to this community member, verbal and physical abuse by Khalid toward her in front of the children.

Upon arrival to Canada and during a medical screening, Suaad disclosed some concerns about her husband's violent behaviour, although she said that this aggressive behaviour had occurred during the pre-migration period. MRCSSI engaged the mosque where a meeting was held with the family in the presence of the imam and two representatives of the sponsoring group for this refugee family. The imam's presence was positive to the family, and he assured them that they would be receiving support from the Muslim community.

The MRCSSI team identified, in collaboration with the family, the following needs: English-language assessments, medical assessments for all family members, dental services for the children, and an Arabic-speaking life-skill worker/volunteer to support the family. Consequently, the local settlement agency and a health centre were contacted to address these needs.

During her medical assessment, Suaad disclosed some concerns about her husband's violent behaviour, and at this time described it as having occurred during the pre-migration period and continuing post-migration. The health service provider, who was legally obligated to report this disclosure, informed MRCSSI that the child protection service had been notified.

Since the family residence was outside of London, MRCSSI contacted the child protection service in that area to collaborate in ensuring a culturally meaningful intervention. The MRCSSI team and child protection service met jointly with the family. During the visit family conflict escalated when Suaad challenged her husband and asked for separation. She requested support from the attendants with her decision to leave Khalid and be protected from any threats she might be exposed to. The two organizations were very concerned about Suaad and her children's safety, and thus the police were contacted. Upon the arrival of the police, the MRCSSI team members intervened and explained the cultural aspects of the problem and the potential impact of pre-migration experiences on the family in order to facilitate a better understanding of the current family context. The MRCSSI team members also told the police that they believed things were moving in the right direction as the woman and her children were about to leave the house. MRCSSI team members were also careful to avoid escalating the situation by having the police present in the house. The police officers were cooperative and talked with the child protection worker while remaining in their car.

Suaad was provided with two options for herself and her children to ensure their safety: either to be placed in a women's shelter, or to be accommodated in temporary housing offered by the sponsoring group. The MRCSSI team members deliberated the matter with the sponsoring group as they preferred that Suaad and the children be accommodated temporarily in a private house. Suaad agreed to live in the temporary house and also indicated her need for MRCSSI to support her. Khalid agreed to stay in the original family house until further notice. Following this incident, Suaad was enrolled in English-language classes, the children were enrolled in school, and the children were assessed by a children's mental health service provider. Suaad received parenting skills support from a local organization providing in-home support. She and the children began gradually to adapt to their new environment.

Khalid appeared to be overwhelmed by the situation and was very upset. Taking into consideration the pre-migration dramatic stressors combined with the family crisis, MRCSSI referred Khalid for a mental health assessment. The assessor indicated that, throughout the interview, Khalid was not forthcoming and tended to normalize his experiences. Because of this, they did not rule out a PTSD diagnosis. The mental health assessor noted that Khalid's belief system regarding women was very rigid and that he articulated this very clearly. The assessment indicated that this attitude was an underlying factor in his controlling and violent behaviour toward his wife.

The social worker at MRCSSI worked closely with the family and assisted Suaad and her children in this early stage of refugee settlement and integration. At the same time, they worked with Khalid in taking steps to change his attitude toward women and to acquire effective communication skills and positive behaviour. MRCSSI, early in their work with the family, had initiated a formal collaborative multi-organizational intervention and informal support from the ethno-cultural community that ensured a support system surrounding the family. The CORT meetings resulted in engaging and facilitating needed services, and adapting service delivery to meet the unique needs of the family. The MRCSSI team attempted to direct available resources to addressing the challenges faced by the family as a result of their traumatic pre-migration experiences. They assisted Suaad and her children in adjusting to their new environment, and supported Khalid in addressing his violent behaviour and adopting a healthy attitude in his relationship with Suaad and their children without putting them at further risk. At the same time, they paid careful attention to not contributing to further isolating Khalid as this would exacerbate his response to previous trauma and current post-migration adaptation.

As service providers who had been engaged to this point, we at MRCSSI would say that the most important outcome of the CIFSR process to that date was interrupting the escalation of violence that could lead to critical tragedies during the initial response period. The mother and her children left home safely following the mother's disclosure and request for assistance. The father was engaged with supportive services to help manage risk and prevent further isolation and associated escalation of risk. Further services and support for the whole family had been mapped out through the CORT process.

Reflections from Mohammed

The family had experienced war, internal displacement, loss of family members, and forced migration to a nearby country before their arrival in Canada. They suffered prolonged trauma during their pre-migration journey. They came to Canada as privately sponsored refugees and lived in a rural area. The family was isolated from their ethno-cultural community. Utilizing FAST provided the MRCSSI social worker with an in-depth understanding of the family context and the various aspects that interplay as risk factors to family safety. In this case, assessing the cultural aspect revealed a level of rigidity that resulted in Khalid assaulting Suaad within a month of their arrival. This understanding then informed early interventions that took this rigidity into account.

The results of the FAST helped MRCSSI to invite the child protection agency and the police to act in a less intrusive manner. Everyone involved in the case agreed to listen to MRCSSI's voice, and despite the fact that this case would be considered as a high-risk case, we were able to deal with it as an early intervention. Our meetings with the child protection worker resulted in the worker agreeing to meet with the family for education and not for investigation in order to reduce possible anxiety of the family and encourage them to cooperate. We also asked the police not to appear in front of the family as we were negotiating to move the mother and her children from the family home to a safe place. The police agreed to support our plan. The results of our FAST assessment, showing that the violence could be situational and very much related to the pre-migration trauma and cultural differences of the perpetrator, assisted us in communicating clearly with the involved services.

MRCSSI initiated a multi-organizational intervention that engaged mandated and non-mandated organizations and brought them together through several CORT and case conference meetings. These meetings allowed for the implementation of CIFSR-guided interventions that supported the family in addressing some of the most immediately critical risk factors in a culturally meaningful manner. MRCSSI team members were able to work with both partners separately and this provided Suaad and her children with a safe living space during these early stages of settlement and integration. At the same time, MRCSSI supported Khalid to be responsible for his actions, to address his abusive behaviour, and to seek positive changes. At this point he was embracing change slowly by gaining a better understanding and appreciation of both the law and dominant cultural norms in Canada. One strategy that MRCSSI used in engaging with Khalid was to help him be in touch with his new reality in Canada. Khalid, as a man brought up in a patriarchal society, had difficulty accepting that his authority as a man was challenged within the Canadian culture. Our engagement involved what I would call "establishing a base for reasonable conversation," and I see this as a very important mark of progress. I am referring here to our encouragement for him to gradually acknowledge and accept the new context in which he was living, and to seek help and guidance in adapting his own behaviour to these expectations. This understanding includes the fact that any potential danger toward his children will not in any way be tolerated, and that physical violence toward his wife is not at all acceptable.

What community service providers have to say...

"MRCSSI was invaluable on several levels. Case formulation through a culturally competent lens aided the clinical interventions and ongoing assessment of needs. In many respects MRCSSI offered a culture brokerage role in helping both the family and us gain a better understanding of mutual expectations in the therapy process. Additionally, they were available for many cases to provide adjunctive therapy, i.e., parent support, individual counselling for the parent, and marital counselling. It was incredibly beneficial to have the opportunity for MRCSSI staff to join family therapy sessions, and collaborate as a team with the family. Their presence at case conferences on very complex cases has, again, provided a relevant clinical, culturally competent perspective that helped to guide discussion and recommendations especially in cases involving violence."

(Community service provider)

"Cross-training opportunities were a good start. A commitment to 'tough it out' through difficult and complex cases is essential. Completing these cases together cements the relationships, and provides insight on both sides that cannot be gained through training alone. Debriefing after a case concludes is a valuable learning tool. Mutual respect for each agency's values and needs must be maintained."

(Community service provider)

"The cases that we have referred have been very complicated and some have been extremely high risk. The outcomes were remarkable – families which were in crisis were stabilized – often in ways that we did not anticipate but worked well for them. We tend to approach domestic violence from a risk management perspective that requires families to be separated and men to become more isolated. This creates risk. The manner in which MRCSSI intervenes ensures that the man is more supported (versus more isolated) and that the dynamic risk factors that he presents with are better managed. This same strategy works across the board and we have learned a great deal from it. More evidence – less children in care!"

(Community service provider)

6 Culturally Informed Models of Responses to Family Violence in Collectivist Communities

Family violence is not a familiar concept for many newcomers and other visible minorities in North American or predominantly Western societies, especially those coming from collectivist backgrounds. In many cultures, conflicts that could lead to violence between intimate partners or between parents and their children are considered private family matters that should be dealt with through traditional cultural means. Collectivist cultures tend to keep any family conflicts within the family and treat these as family secrets, morally obliging everyone in the family to not share information about them with outsiders. In these circumstances, family members are most likely to first seek guidance from elders of the extended family or leaders in the faith or ethno-cultural community. Usually the focus of the solution is preserving the family, and not necessarily resolving the conflict as that might lead to separation and divorce. In a collectivist context, it is a common practice for an abused woman to take her children and go to her family when she experiences abuse by her husband. Her family would then talk with her husband or her husband's family and come up with a safety plan to protect her from any further victimization along with some compensation. Following this practice, newcomer females in Canada, whose family members are not nearby, would usually talk with their friends or neighbours about problems they are having with their husbands, including incidents of abuse. These women may be encouraged by these support persons to go to shelters or call the police, or they may directly choose to ask for outside help from shelters or the police. Women in these circumstances would typically expect that someone would tell their husbands to stop the violence and ask them to respect their wives. However, they would not expect that their male partners would be arrested or forced to stay away from the family. In many cases when women from collectivist communities do choose to go to a shelter, they will soon choose to return home where they are more vulnerable and continue living within an abusive situation. According to Baldev Mutta (CEO, Punjabi Community Health Services, Brampton, Ontario, Canada – informal communication), South Asian women will avoid going to shelters because they see women's shelters as encouraging divorce and they want to avoid the associated stigma attached to marital dissolution.

It is important to understand that women are not necessarily unaware of their rights and the services available to support and protect them from their partner's abuse. In spite of their awareness, however, many women from collectivist cultures are hesitant to use established social support services in the broader community because they fear becoming isolated from their own community and other family members. Understanding and considering the cultural context of family violence and intervention challenges can help broaden our perspective to better understand the dilemma of women and children from collectivist backgrounds who are at risk of or victimized by domestic violence, and, accordingly, to consider alternatives for providing them with meaningful services and support.

In this chapter we talk about culturally adapted intervention programs through an analysis of the Culturally Integrative Family Safety Response (CIFSR) in comparison with other culturally informed models of intervention with families involved with family violence. I (Mohammed) will also share my personal reflections in working with both established services in the Canadian mainstream and directly with Muslim communities to address and respond to family violence in a culturally meaningful way.

The first time I (Mohammed) felt that there was a real need to revise and re-examine what we consider to be culturally appropriate or informed family violence intervention was in 2002. At that time, I was working on a small research project funded by the Centre for Research and Education on Violence Against Women and Children at Western University in London, Ontario. The recommendations coming out of this research were to build bridges between anti-violence agencies and the local Muslim community in order to reduce gaps in services for victims of family violence in this community. Two local organizations, the London Coordinating Committee to End Woman Abuse and Changing Ways, an agency working with abusive men, supported these recommendations.

My research was about barriers to accessing services for Muslim abused women. Some of these women were likely underutilizing established community-based services because of fear of isolation from their community. At the same time, existing service providers were concerned that local Muslim religious leaders were not pro-women and were favouring men in giving support and direction at the time of family conflict or when women came forward to identify family violence. Both the broader Muslim community's reaction and the concerns expressed by many of the local religious leaders when women left marital relationships were often negative. These responses included blaming women for bringing shame to the family and for abandoning the family unit while attempting to find a solution for themselves at the cost of the family.

Similarly, I heard some misunderstandings and misconceptions held by service providers about the religion of Islam and assumptions that women would be advised by religious leaders or community elders/leaders to not leave abusive relationships based on Sharia law. This was a very sensitive topic during this period of time because of the debate in Ontario about Sharia-based arbitration that followed an announcement from the Islamic Institute of Civil Justice that they intended to begin offering Sharia-based services in Ontario (see Korteweg & Selby, 2012, for more in-depth discussion of this issue). The provincial government originally stated qualified support for this, but eventually banned religious arbitration of family law concerns. The public debate, involving Muslim and non-Muslim voices, extended beyond provincial boundaries and attracted worldwide attention (Korteweg & Selby, 2012). I believe it is not unusual, based on my involvement in working with many established service providers in the broader community, for risk assessments and responses to family violence within particular collectivist communities to be influenced by these broader discourses and service providers' stereotypical attitudes that men's violence against women is tolerated by particular cultures and endorsed by the teachings of Islam and Sharia law.

I heard during my research that, from the perspective of established service-providing organizations, increasing community awareness about their services and enhancing their frontline workers' cross-cultural communication skills would lead to an increase in the number of women from marginalized communities seeking out their services. These organizations also stated that more women would access their resources if someone could speak to faith and community leaders in predominantly Muslim ethno-cultural communities about their obligation to protect vulnerable women and their children. In my view, these proposed solutions, focused as they were on community defi-cits, missed the equal importance of examining whether or not, and to what extent, the service delivery model itself was meeting the needs of diverse cultural groups.

As someone who works with existing broader community-based services in the area of family violence, and who is also a member of the Arab and Muslim community, I could see the struggle both groups were experiencing, and the challenges they were facing in coming up with solutions that con-sidered core cultural values of victims without compromising their safety. I could also see strengths and opportunities that sometimes were missed by both groups.

I see the main problem as not just the barrier to accessing services, but rather the dilemma faced by abused women in collectivist, immigrant com-munities that prevents them from asking for outside help. If this dilemma is not recognized or understood properly, it is most likely that the risk assess-ment will not be accurate and, if this is the case, the incorrectly labelled "problem" will lead to an inadequately determined "intervention." Similarly, failing to recognize the complexities of the dilemma faced by women in asking for outside help will contribute to poorly specified research questions that may overlook underlying concerns or contributing factors. When the problem is framed as cultural and language barrier only, the proposed solutions address a perceived deficiency in the cultural community (i.e., the members of this community are lacking a certain knowledge, language, or understanding that would allow them to access our services, so we need to translate or educate them in order to have them access our services). An alternative view would consider how service providers' policies and practices themselves may be contributing to inaccessibility.

A question that arises in discussions and research questions regarding the challenges of working with women from collectivist backgrounds is whether they prefer to go to service providers in the broader community or culturally based services. This preference may depend on each woman's particular and current context. Based on my observation, I would say that a woman who comes from a religiously based oppression experience is more likely to not ask for help from a service that is affiliated with a cultural and/or religious community. Conversely, there are many women who identify themselves as women of faith and who hold their cultural heritage as an important identity marker. These women are most likely to look for services or supports that are faith and/or culturally based. Similarly, beliefs about gender roles, marriage, and authority (Hancock, Ames, & Behnke, 2014) can all influence women's decision making or preferences for where or how to seek direction, guidance, or support. Given the importance of context, it is important to not assume that all women from collectivist, Muslim, or Arab communities will be driven by the same impetus in accessing supports, services, and resources in their broader or local community when they are facing risk or violence in their homes.

Lisa Goodman and Deborah Epstein (2005) make a compelling argument for the ways in which the current American system that focuses primarily on mandatory responses to the batterer (arrest, prosecution, counselling programs), while laudable in terms of underlining that the state will not condone violence against women, does not necessarily address the diverse needs of victims of domestic violence. They describe in some detail how "no single response can meet the needs of every woman, and many responses that are well suited to one circumstance can worsen another" (Goodman & Epstein, 2005). They also point to inflexible policy as being particularly problematic for serving the needs of marginalized groups such as immigrant and racialized minority women. They provide examples of programs that are more responsive to the needs of women who are victims of family violence by incorporating more collaborative relationships between various parts of the judicial system to amplify the voice of victims, training community leaders to provide tangible supports for victims, and enhancing advocacy efforts.

There are at least three different approaches to culturally adapted family violence intervention. Differences between these approaches are based on how family violence in distinct cultural communities and related service-providing groups is understood and conceptualized. The two approaches we wish to discuss here are culturally sensitive and faith or culturally based.

We recognize that terms such as "culturally sensitive" or "culturally based" have been defined and used in a number of ways across and within various disciplines, and that the definition of culture itself is contested. We do not intend to lay a particular claim or certainty to the terms we have chosen here. We use them for descriptive and comparative purposes only. A discussion of the various uses and merits of terminology in conceptualizing, and indeed in researching organizational models for the provision of social services, is beyond the scope of our presentation here.

Culturally Sensitive Approaches

Culturally sensitive approaches focus on enhancing cross-cultural communication between established services and diverse cultural clients. These practices are often introduced by established service agencies in the interest of implementing diversity policies for community-based victim services or family violence services, and improving their level of cultural competency in order to respond to rapidly changing demographics. The levels of flexibility and cultural adaptability associated with these approaches depend on many factors. For example, mandated services such as police services and the justice system have difficulties introducing flexibility. More informal services can be more flexible and adaptable. The underlying assumptions for these approaches within more traditional service organizations is that broader community-based services are well equipped to serve any group and their workers are, or can be, trained to deliver their services in a culturally sensitive manner. Often a culturally sensitive approach relies heavily on the use of interpreters, the provision of training in cultural sensitivity for frontline workers, and outreach to diverse cultural communities in order to raise awareness about their services, the rights of women, gender equality, and the legal consequences of family violence. Organizations may also take steps to hire visible-minority individuals who speak different languages beyond English or French (the official languages in a Canadian context). In order to support these measures to increase cultural sensitivity, more public resources are directed to established community-based organizations for activities such as interpretation and public education, for example. The organizations adopting culturally sensitive approaches include many of the service providers that would be involved with immigrant families when a perpetrator has been charged or when child protection concerns are raised, and who provide support for victims as part of their interventions.

An example of a service-providing organization utilizing a culturally sensitive approach with flexibility and cultural adaptability is the Multilingual Orientation Service Association for Immigrant Communities (MOSAIC) in British Columbia, Canada. MOSAIC provides culturally sensitive, multilingual services for immigrants and refugees with regard to issues related to integration and settlement. MOSAIC provides services such as interpretation and translation, family counselling, settlement programs, legal advocacy, and programs for seniors, in addition to programs directed at domestic violence and victim services. Their Forced Marriage program, for example, aims to raise community awareness about forced marriages as a form of gender-based violence. MOSAIC and its collaborating partners in Forced Marriage use a risk assessment framework specifically designed to assist providers in dealing with cases of forced marriage (for further information, see www.endforcedmarriages.ca, oriented to providing resources for people facing forced marriages as well as service providers). In a program similar to Muslim Resource Centre for Social Support and Integration (MRCSSI)'s Reclaim Honour initiative, MOSAIC launched a project in collaboration with immigrant-serving agencies entitled Preventing and Reducing Violence Against Women and Girls in the Name of "Honour"; this project is directed at promoting awareness on the issue of violence against women and deconstructing the concept of "honour-based violence." Both initiatives use interactive dialogues to create a safe environment for girls and women to come forward with concerns they have, work to decrease risks and perceived barriers to speaking out, and provide opportunities for service providers to gain insight into the community's cultural norms and enhance their cultural sensitivity. Multicultural Victim Services through MOSAIC provides client-centred services for victims of all types of crime, including violence against women. These services are delivered in a client's native language and provide information about safety assessment and planning for a broad range of individuals, groups, and communities. In summary, MOSAIC is one example of an established social service organization responding to family violence in a culturally sensitive manner. Their focus is to overcome language and cultural barriers by providing services to immigrants and refugees in their mother language and with visible-minority professionals.

Faith and Culturally Based Approaches

Where culturally sensitive approaches might be seen as primarily adopted by existing services in order to address potential barriers and extend services to specific communities, faith or culturally based approaches could be seen as the means by which localized communities attempt to address similar problems of access to services. Introducing culturally sensitive practices that are directly targeting a specific cultural or ethnic community, for example Muslim communities, may in effect be saying that certain cultural groups themselves are part of the problem that creates barriers to access. In fact, service providers may see the collectivist community's emphasis on preserving the family unit as evidence of their competing objectives, and therefore not initiate partnership building with respective community leaders. If a similar view of competing interests is held at the local community level, or if service-providing organizations are viewed as holding negative attitudes toward particular religious or cultural values, then the religious or cultural communities themselves may initiate and endorse faith or culturally based approaches to supporting members of these communities. Faith and culturally based approaches may also be developed by these communities in response to what local community members see as intrusive interventions based on the dominant culture's values in cases of family violence. Collectivist community members may also think that supporting women and children at the cost of the collective interest of the family will lead to family breakdown and the humiliation of men. Based on these assumptions, the faith or cultural community may build their own response to family violence within their communities. The focus of these kinds of initiatives is primarily on preserving the family and encouraging women and children to find solutions to their safety concerns without leaving their homes or their community in cases of family violence. They are oriented to the belief that they can support the victims or those who are at risk without separation and negatively impacting family unity.

The strengths of faith and culturally based approaches to addressing violence within local communities are that subtler or more complex aspects of community values and day-to-day life, beyond language and what can be taught to those outside of the community's traditions, can be integrated directly into the provision of supports and programs. There are women who are reluctant to go to a women's shelter or involve police in a family matter when they experience domestic violence. Men from collectivist backgrounds may find it difficult to talk about their attitudes and behaviours, especially violent actions, in a group setting. This will particularly be the case when others in the group are from the dominant culture in which systemic racism exists and may be quick to judge or see these disclosures as confirming negative stereotypes. At the same time, however, there will be women and families who are not comfortable using faith and culturally based services because they don't want to be recognized within their community of origin as having family problems, especially those related to family violence.

An example of a culturally based program is Punjabi Community Health Services (PCHS) in Peel Region, Ontario, Canada. This organization began as a community development project in 1990. They identified the need to address concerns related to addictions, violence against women, and family breakdown. Their services include those designed to improve healthy family interactions, assistance related to mental illness and substance use, settlement, seniors' programs, and community development. Baldev Mutta, CEO of PCHS, talks about the value for clients of seeing professionals who not only speak their language, but who also understand the day-to-day life of being a member of this community (2015, informal communication). He also provides an illustration of the importance of understanding the collectivist community and distinctions that may be lost on someone operating within a more individualist understanding of how to address conflict. He says (2015, informal communication) that, "in many collectivist cultures, conflict is inherent in marriage," indeed in most relationships, and that because of this, "the framework for responding to conflicts is mediation rather than resolution." If conflict is ever-present in some form, then the goal, based on collectivist principles, is to mediate and provide skills in managing conflict, rather than having a goal of resolving it. He further remarked that he sees "the current framework for addressing domestic violence in Canada is through conflict resolution. This leads to separating those who are at risk or victimized by the violence from those who perpetuate the violence and represent risk to others." According to Mutta, this separation doesn't then allow for mediation or supporting family members in finding new ways to respond to the conflict in their lives:

> So these are totally different concepts of conflict and accordingly different ways of responding to them. Within a collectivist context, the response is more about mediation, which means that the expectation is that both individuals involved in the conflict are not just representing themselves but also their extended families and tribes. The expectation being that you have to learn to live with it and not necessarily to look for solutions for yourself only.

This fuller understanding of conflict mediation leads to different interventions that support families in finding new ways to interact while still maintaining safety.

Summary

We have described herein some of the more common ways that service providers and communities have approached developing services for marginalized families experiencing family violence. We see that both culturally sensitive and faith and culturally based approaches are successful in enhancing accessibility to services and meeting the needs of diverse families. While there are some similarities between these approaches and CIFSR, there are some key differences. The similarities entail carefully crafting services, supports, resources, and interventions to meet the needs of family members experiencing family violence who are from diverse communities. We support and appreciate the varied ways in which people in distress can be assisted, and the many doorways for entry to service that exist in many communities. There is a significant difference between CIFSR and the other two approaches with regard to initiating, building, and maintaining relationships across sectors to more fully support families. These relationships allow for the engagement and support of established service providers, cultural organizations, and the leaders of marginalized collectivist communities. It is this relationship building and the collaborative practices that attend coordinated responses that set the CIFSR model somewhat apart. Early bridging of services and collectivist communities can be facilitated by a cultural organization such as MRCSSI. These initial steps serve to build awareness and promote education for service providers and community members. As the relationships and awareness develop further, opportunities arise to inform each other's activities, with increased knowledge within services and for community members contributing to improvements in delivery and awareness, as well as enhanced supports for families. Further along in time and experience, and as complex family situations are brought to the fore, there are opportunities to use this extended knowledge and firmer relationships to engage in and support the more nuanced responses required from multiple actors within mandated and non-mandated organizations and groups. As an example, we provide here a description of some key aspects of an early program developed by MRCSSI.

The Safe Integration Project (SIP) was one of MRCSSI's first attempts to put the preliminary ideas of CIFSR into practice. The SIP was developed to address and respond to family violence within families coming from conflict zones (countries of origin in which there was war and political conflict). This was a joint program with the Cross Cultural Learner Centre, a settlement agency in London, Ontario. Our goal was to identify risk factors of family violence in these families as early as possible so that we could intervene in the early stage of family conflict. Because of our early involvement with families at risk we were able to prevent family violence and interrupt escalation of family conflict. A key component of the SIP was that we also worked to engage key existing services from the broader community with these families before the situation became critical. We not only worked to ensure the engagement of other services, but we regularly brought together the various players – settlement workers, those working with the adults as well as the school-aged children in the families, social workers from schools and other facilities in which family members were involved, family physicians, and other healthcare professionals working with the family – and talked together about the family system, and aspects of the broader system that were or were not well connected or coordinated with the SIP-related services. We received feedback from the frontline service providers and managers within these organizations that the enhanced knowledge about what had gone on for these families and their cultural context, what was happening now for all family members (particularly for those providers who were working with only one or two family members), and the ability to coordinate actions and planning for ongoing supports was invaluable. These relationships and coordinated actions provided for the least intrusive and most well-supported involvement, when required, of mandated services such as police and the child protection agency. MRCSSI maintained connection with the other organizations involved, and arranged for local community engagement when that was deemed useful, and the family counsellor at MRCSSI was able to provide ongoing support to families to navigate and understand the involvement of various other services. The outcome of this program was very positive and successful, not least because of the relationships initiated and maintained, the knowledge sharing and educational opportunities for all, and coordinated planning and action. We see these as important and valuable extensions to other models of cultural sensitivity and awareness.

7 Training Implications

In this chapter, we extend the lessons we have learned from family members, service providers, and our own experience of putting these ideas into practice, and describe the training implications we see. These training ideas are directed to educators who are training new professionals, as well as in-service trainers providing ongoing training for more advanced professionals who have been working in the fields of family violence, child welfare, and family safety for a longer period of time. We also discuss in this chapter our ideas about providing support for service providers across organizational systems.

Educating New Professionals (From Lynda's Perspective)

As an educator working in a post-secondary educational institution and training master's level family therapists, I find the fit between what we learn from practicing within the Culturally Integrative Family Safety Response (CIFSR) model and a relational/systemic approach to working with individuals, couples, and families to be very exciting. Tailoring interventions to a marginalized and minority-status community's cultural context is a key step in attending to the broader systemic influences on persons' and families' lives. Widening that cultural lens to incorporate the ways in which collectivist principles and values may run up against more prominent individualist approaches in a North American and specifically Canadian context is, I believe, particularly informative. It is important to understand the ways in which the mainstream or more established community-based system is organized to privilege certain ways of working, based on the primacy of individual rights. For example, this lens influences how interventions with victims and perpetrators of violent acts, persons struggling with the effects of pre-migration trauma and the disruption of extended family and community relationships, and members of specific religious communities or ethno-cultural groups are constructed. This is a prime example of how to explicitly identify systemic influences on our practices at organizational as well as face-to-face levels. Unpacking these assumptions and practices is valuable for early professionals as they consider their own approaches to working with various populations. Developing new ways of forming what I like to think of as "collectives" of practitioners and community leaders (collaborative groups oriented to working with collectivist practices or principles and surrounding a family with formal and informal supports and services) as implemented by Mohammed Baobaid and his colleagues and partners over the past decade or more, provides an excellent example of expanding organizational and professional practices in response to these challenges. I see these shifts in practice as pointing to new best-practice options for individual practitioners and organizations. As a family therapist training new systemic and relational psychotherapists, I appreciate the object lesson in the importance of relationship building at the organizational level and across communities, as well as explicit attention to the relational context, pre- and post-migration influences, and the social fabric of the families with whom we work.

The ideas informing CIFSR practices specifically lend themselves well to teaching new professionals. I write here primarily with regard to training relational and systemic psychotherapists who are working with newcomers and members of non-mainstream communities with collectivist traditions and roots, and with particular emphasis on concerns related to family violence, pre-migration trauma, and child welfare. I'm sure that you, the reader, will see ways in which these ideas can be extended to training in related professions associated with child welfare, immigrant and refugee settlement, health care, employment services, education, court-related supports, domestic violence programs and shelters, and community development.

The CIFSR model provides an excellent scaffold for teaching and learning relational, culturally sensitive practices with families and individuals. In particular, the Four Aspects Screening Tool (FAST) assessment can be used to ensure full attention to various aspects of a person's and family's relationships and interactions with others. These include ethnic, cultural, and religious background and influences; factors based in the local and broader community that are affecting family safety; alongside historical and current experiences related to collectivist perspectives, pre- and post-migration history and context, local social interactions, and connections with leaders/champions who support family safety. Similarly, the Coordinated Organizational Response Teams (CORT) constellation of relevant organizations and community/family supports provides a framework for considering the structural and systemic elements of a person's or family's day-to-day life and safety.

As a family therapy supervisor and professor, I have taught students how to use genograms and systemic mapping tools collaboratively with clients over many years. Working together with the Muslim Resource Centre for Social Support and Integration (MRCSSI) and the broader range of community service providers involved in working with families within the CIFSR model has allowed me to see the value of using genograms and mapping systemic influences visually with a group of service providers aiming to support a family's safety and well-being. I have appreciated the opportunity to see broader applications of these tools in helping to contextualize individual family members' struggles and behaviour, and to consider the broader family system and interactions with the collectivist community. Particularly when a service provider may be engaged with only one person or one context in which the family operates, this richer description of how the overall family interacts and what supports or hinders positive change can be a real asset to group support for family safety.

Similarly, providing examples of how other professionals may view a family or an issue of concern can be quite instructive for novice or early-career professionals. Consider, for example, the potentially divergent perspectives of a school social worker involved with adolescent children, a physician working with their mother, and police or court personnel involved with charges pending against their father, alongside a more comprehensive picture of family interactions in a cultural context provided by the CIFSR. This reflection on various perspectives allows for a fuller understanding not only of the family interactions and individual actions, but also of how and why various systems may be responding in the way that they are. Consideration of case assessment and interventions at this broader macro level provides excellent opportunities to think about how one might, as a service provider, collaborate with others in assessment and intervention for family safety and well-being.

It is evident in what we have written so far about the CIFSR model that one of the unique aspects of working in this way is the relationship building across organizations and service sectors in the mainstream and mentors and champions in the more marginalized collectivist community. Highlighting the importance of these relationships, and the time required to build and sustain them, is, we believe, a valuable exercise in understanding and intervening to support families in collectivist and non-mainstream communities. It does, at the same time, provide new learning opportunities in training programs for early professionals. Considering the challenges of bridging cultures, sectors, professions, and communities is an important aspect of culturally integrative practices. This should be incorporated into early training and ongoing professional development, and provides an opportunity to extend learning beyond cultural sensitivity to actions that promote cross-sector and cross-cultural dialogue, and sensitive support for change and enhanced safety from a collectivist perspective. Building awareness from the beginning about the time commitment that will attend this practice, and appreciation for the value of investing this time, will augment professional training and development in a culturally integrative manner.

CIFSR Training with Practitioners (From Mohammed's Perspective)

Training frontline service providers and managers in mainstream organizations, in addition to serving as an important aspect of the community and clinical work at MRCSSI, has informed the development of the CIFSR model. The feedback MRCSSI has received from professionals working in child welfare, police forces, schools, medical clinics, settlement agencies, and court systems has indicated that the training advances their practice skills, as does participating in the CIFSR model of practice. The protocols that we have developed with a local child protection agency, for example, have informed ongoing training and practices in other communities and across different organizations. We continue to hear that training related to the use of FAST and CORT approaches to assessment and intervention is valuable to frontline service providers in their CIFSR work and their clinical work more generally. We believe that this training contributes to conceptualizing family safety more systemically and working more collaboratively in a range of contexts. Similarly, we hear at the organizational and community level that this type of training and collaboration, when it brings together key partners or potential partners in a specific community, is supportive of ongoing community development.

MRCSSI provides training sessions aimed at supporting service providers to develop effective approaches that respond to family violence, including "honour-based" violence and forced marriages, within collectivist contexts. We illustrate the CIFSR approach by using MRCSSI's experiences working collaboratively with stakeholders in responding to the needs of victims of family violence in collectivist communities. When we train groups of professionals in the use of FAST and CORT, for example, we begin by providing a history of the CIFSR approach and conceptualizations of family violence within families from collectivist backgrounds. We share the goals of CIFSR and describe how FAST and CORT fit into the model and practice approach. We highlight the unique aspects of each part of the model. Our overall goals of training sessions are to:

- Orient and enhance service providers' knowledge of the cultural context and needs of families from collectivist communities.
- Increase knowledge and understanding of the unique aspects, practical applications, and anticipated outcomes of FAST and CORT.
- Increase service providers' confidence and ability to engage in the early stages of family conflict, resulting in better adaptability of services and early identification and intervention with conflicts.
- Increase service providers' capacity to respond to the complex needs of individuals and families within collectivist cultural communities.
- Build trusting relationships with multidisciplinary professionals with the expressed hope that this will lead to more collaborative and integrative prevention and intervention responses to family violence.

Our training often involves using case-based and small-group approaches to learning. This allows us to assess where participants are at in their own understanding and positioning, and opens up possibilities for greater synthesis of learning material and enhanced practical implications when engaging in group dialogue. We utilize interactive training in order to help participants find commonalities across their various practice backgrounds, and work to utilize a shared vision and unique problem solving when working in small groups. The individual and group exercises that we use are intended to engage and be inclusive of all types of learning styles and personalities. This approach also allows us to determine whether participants are engaged in the material and when we are conveying the material in a way that is easily digestible.

In both FAST and CORT training at MRCSSI we provide background theoretical and conceptual rationales for the two approaches. We share their history, purpose, and objectives. We present detailed descriptions with case examples and anticipated outcomes. In our training sessions, we look for:

- Participant engagement in the material.
- Questions asked by participants – the more complex the question, the more we know we have created a safe space for engaging in possibilities.
- Richness and depth of discussions during case-based exercises and debriefing of various interactive exercises.
- Ongoing feedback as to whether we are clear and whether participants are able to "see themselves" in this work and buy into this practice approach.

We know that we have been successful when we receive formal feedback in response to questionnaires we provide at the end of training. We also judge success in terms of new partnerships with service providers, more consultation requests and visits, and increased referrals.

We have learned from the feedback to these training events that many participants look forward to future opportunities to either engage in further training with their colleagues and community partners, or to build consultation groups and opportunities into their future collaborative practices. The training that we have provided so far has been evolving and we still learn from the feedback we receive about ways we can improve. Participants across sectors and in various roles at service-providing organizations ask that training content be practical and use the professional service language with which they are familiar. Our training can be tailored to provide the whole CIFSR package, or specific parts of the approach to meet the needs of a particular group or service sector. For example, settlement services are looking for a small and easy-to-use screening tool that will help them identify risk factors of family violence during their initial screening process with newly arrived refugees. They also look for tools and training that help them respond to warning signs of family violence without necessarily involving the police if the situation is not yet critical. Mandated services such as the police, child protection, and victim services have less flexibility in their protocols, and are more interested in training that will enhance their cross-cultural communication with their clients.

The CIFSR model, as we have developed it in our context, principally promotes collaboration that rests on a strong role for a culturally based organization such as MRCSSI. The intent is to empower and engage culturally diverse groups directly as part of interventions with families at risk and in developing community solutions through working collaboratively with established service providers. Such an organization is not always well positioned, at least initially, to take on such a key role in a community. In our case, MRCSSI acts as a cultural broker between service providers and the Muslim community, and also provides trained professionals who can work within the CIFSR and conduct a FAST assessment to support and augment mainstream services. This facilitates more equal partnerships with other service providers and coordinated responses. In instances where a cultural organization is newly forming or does not yet have the capacity for providing such services, the CIFSR approach and the FAST assessment can also be used by existing community-based service providers who are interested in providing a culturally meaningful response to family violence. In these cases, the service providers will expect to have something that is easy to integrate with their well-established risk assessment tools and intervention models.

We see training in this model as complementary to other types of training at an agency or community level, such as culturally sensitive training with the anti-oppression framework. Anti-oppressive practices and positioning ensure that services do not exclude marginalized groups. Such training further enhances practitioners' understanding of the cultural background of a diversity of clients and reduces barriers to accessing services. We see, however, that training in this model can support mandated service providers who may be more limited in their flexibility with regard to risk assessment strategies and responses to newcomer and refugee families. We recognize that service providers can easily become overwhelmed with the stories told by families and individuals impacted by pre-migration trauma and post-migration stressors, and that this may lead them to fall back on stricter adherence to policies and procedures. We believe that training in CIFSR and FAST can help service providers see other alternatives beyond intrusive interventions oriented around individual safety, and risk assessments that are not designed to illuminate the influences of living in conflict zones and migration-related trauma and disruption, as well as illuminating specific cultural aspects of collectivist communities. During CIFSR-based training, participants are encouraged to use screening tools that are culturally meaningful without compromising their legislated mandates and that protect the safety of those who are most vulnerable. We see that CIFSR-based training does not replicate existing training in cultural sensitivity, but rather complements it by enhancing practitioners' cultural capacity to better respond to the needs of collectivist families, particularly those who have migrated from conflict zones and who are at risk of experiencing family violence.

We would like to develop future training that incorporates the use of case examples with even more intention. We see that examples of families' experiences and CIFSR-guided responses assist participants' understanding of the complexity of cases involving pre-and post-migration stressors together with a range of other factors. One ongoing challenge for us is to consider how we use concrete case examples to better understand key factors related to a set of unique family and community circumstances together with case-specific CIFSR-guided responses, while at the same time not under-representing the model's complexity. Practitioners and agencies are often primarily interested in how to use specific tools that will help them be culturally sensitive in their interventions without compromising their established policies and procedures. This is understandable from a perspective of considering their heavy workload, liability, the challenges of working with high-risk situations, and the wide range of practice experience across an agency's staff. However, simplifying too much or focusing only on certain aspects of the model can get in the way of considering the potentially greater benefits associated with broader organizational and system-wide practices that could enhance responses to families in marginalized cultural communities more generally. As we continue to use case examples in our training, we want to integrate facilitated strategies to deepen conversations and identify further opportunities for strengthening collaborative practice and responses. Our hope is that participants in these processes will not only understand how CIFSR and FAST work, but that they will also contribute to enriching the CIFSR model while they are implementing it.

At this time, at MRCSSI we are also working on a project focused on strengthening the broader community's capacity for implementing CIFSR and creating safe environments for women and girls in Muslim communities who are experiencing violence. We are considering the development of an ongoing working group that would consist of clinical managers from various organizations, including Muslim community organizations. We have also thought about the potential benefits of a working group or means of enhancing communication at the level of frontline service practitioners. We see this working group as meeting regularly, perhaps for monthly lunch meetings, and providing a context in which to develop and enhance the necessary relationships, knowledge, and capacities for working together and engaging in collaborative responses. These reflective and inter-professional dialogues will serve to extend and further develop the CIFSR model and practices.

Engaging in Community Development (From Mohammed's Perspective)

Similar to the training of service-providing professionals, MRCSSI staff members have also been engaged, as described earlier (see Chapter 3), in building community awareness in the area of family violence and safety-related issues. This training has involved leaders of Muslim communities from faith-based groups as well as ethno-cultural groups, students, and women's groups. It is very challenging to cover all of the diverse groups within Muslim communities. Based on MRCSSI's community mapping, we have identified key groups in our local community and work to ensure that at least two major groups, reflecting faith and ethno-cultural groups, are represented in all of our community engagement activities.

Specific approaches we have used include informal community conversations in familiar gathering places such as mosques, Islamic centres, and ethno-cultural clubs. These conversations have helped us to establish relationships with respective communities and set the stage for more formal community capacity-building activities. MRCSSI is invited to these groups and to their gathering spaces as their guest. We act as facilitators for awareness raising unique to each community, for example, on issues related to family relations and family conflicts. Our intentions in these activities are to initiate bridge building between the local community and established service providers, and to proactively address the potential for miscommunication and misunderstanding that could escalate conflicts between these services and families from this community. We see our role as one of helping community members connect with established services in the broader community in order to get the best advice and consultation. It is not our intent to simply teach them and tell them what they cannot do.

Following these meetings, it is typical for individuals and leaders to agree to participation in future meetings or training activities. In many cases the particular focus for training is requested by local community members, and often these requests include further information about the involvement of the justice system in family conflicts. When we develop our formal training with community leaders we make sure that their voices are represented in the content of the training curriculum. We also use a participatory training approach so that community leaders will continue to have a say in how they want to go forward with the training. Usually we plan day-long training/community-development events that set aside the morning for sharing knowledge and the afternoon for group work using role plays. We also engage different segments of the community in conversation throughout these training activities. Young women, young men, and community leaders including imams, as well as representation from established services in the broader community, would all be part of these training events.

We have learned from community leaders and members that this training is important in several ways. First of all, most of these training activities take place in community settings like mosques or ethno-cultural clubs. We have heard this contributes to community members and leaders feeling that they have an important share in the community development that arises from these events, and they are comfortable with what is shared and discussed. Similarly, these community members and leaders have shared with us that such discussions take away the stigma of addressing sensitive issues like family violence in mosques and other community spaces. The success of these meetings also encourages community leaders and members to encourage others to participate in future training and community development events related to family violence.

We have learned from community leaders and members of the community who are champions of addressing family violence that this community training and awareness-building is important because it dispels many myths about the work of mandated family violence services. This has provided great learning opportunities through discussion of the challenges associated with providing culturally adapted services for Muslim families as well as considering potential solutions and engaging in difficult conversations where everyone's voice is respected. The result of this community development work is a better understanding in the local community of how the established system in the broader community works. As well, these activities contribute to developing different and positive ways for community members to work with the more established system and individual service providers.

One thing that many of the local community leaders and members have mentioned is the importance and value of enhancing their understanding of warning signs of family violence as well as knowing what they can do rather than waiting until the situation escalates and becomes more critical. They say that they now know their obligation is to protect those who seek help from them, that these community members are vulnerable to risk of violence at the time that they are seeking assistance, and that there is real help and support that they can provide, including facilitating connections with appropriate established services in the broader community.

What have training participants had to say?

Responses to a question about what were the "meaningful concepts in training":

> "Importance of early intervention, changing trajectories to influence impact (addressing escalating situations of family violence)."
> "Inclusion of broader family, extended family, religious community, etc."
> "FAST and CORT as valuable tools in range of contexts."
> "Use of 'family safety' versus 'family violence'."

Response to a question about what are seen as "challenges":

> "Limitations to flexibility of incorporating additions to current organization's practices and mandate."

Responses to a question about what participants would "need in order to incorporate [this learning]":

> "follow up workshops"
> "practical experience"
> "supervision"
> "opportunity to discuss and receive constructive feedback"
> "being better equipped to deal with trauma"

Response to a question about what participants found to be the "most valuable part of training":

"I am a 4th year social work student looking to increase my knowledge and skills around cultural competency. This workshop contributed greatly to my understanding of the collectivist nature of various immigrant cultures, of how priorities may differ between individualistic and collectivist cultures, of the stressors immigrant families may be coping with related to their pre- and post-migration experience, and of the value of seeking input and support from significant religious and cultural figures with respect to de-escalating violence within a family. The table activity helped to increase my awareness of how my understanding of domestic violence comes from an individualistic perspective and how this bias impacts my interpretation of and response to families in crisis."

8   What We've Learned and Future Directions

LYNDA: Mohammed, what are some of the highlights for you of what you've learned along the way in developing and nurturing the ideas that have contributed to the Culturally Integrative Family Safety Response (CIFSR)?

MOHAMMED: When I look back at the process of developing and implementing CIFSR, I see different stages and levels of influence. For example, even before the Muslim Resource Centre for Social Support and Integration (MRCSSI) was established in 2009, I was very aware of critical family situations that involved conflict between parents and adolescent daughters in the family. In my position as someone working with a professional social service agency and being from the Muslim and Arab community, I could see more than what was being seen by schools, social services, mental health providers, women's services, and mandated agencies. These girls were trapped between family traditions and the Canadian context, particularly through their experiences at school and being part of the Canadian culture and its mainstream socialization means, including the media. I could see that this was not different from other families coming from a collectivist cultural background and struggling with their adolescent children. I could see also how established service providers were not responding to this "trapped" status for girls and their families. My observations at the time led me to believe that service providers' responses were constrained typically by their policies, procedures, and liabilities that made them respond to any situation like this based on their mandate and not necessarily to the complex needs of these families, including these young women who could at times be at real risk. For example, the criminal justice system response to domestic violence would not take into account the context of domestic violence in newcomer families that could include pre-migration trauma and post-migration stressors. Seeing newcomer men in the context of their history, journey, strengths, and challenges requires that responses are in this context. Responses to men who are themselves survivors of pre-migration trauma and political violence need to be trauma informed. Only after addressing trauma and factors related to migration and cultural difference would existing traditional programs be appropriate.

LYNDA: What has been your experience of our collaboration in writing this book?

MOHAMMED: I have been happy to work on this book with you as it is healing for me. On one hand because we are friends and have been working together for many years and throughout the years you are familiar with my journey. Working with you on this book is like formalizing all the previous conversations that we both thought should come out and be shared with the public. It is, in a sense, safe to gradually lead our conversations and collaboration to this level. It has reminded me of the ethics of this work. Where do we draw the line between protection and sensitivity to complexity? We can't pretend to understand complexities by simplifying the situation we are dealing with. It is important to recognize that any intervention will have big implications for a family. An example I was thinking of was a couple with whom I worked. The refugee-sponsoring group was comprised of caring people. They wanted to help, but their way of seeing what this family was experiencing was not based in the family's reality, which was much more complex than what was on the surface. When I started to work with the family, I saw so many things: illiteracy, physical handicaps, a daughter who had to be married in the refugee camp in order to address an experience of rape, health concerns, and a large family with many children. In this instance, the service providers found the complexity intimidating, and ended up doing further damage as a result of attempting to focus on the needs of only one person and following an established protocol. It is not realistic, for example, within short-term family therapy, to address the very complex underlying issues related to marital or family conflicts. For legally mandated services such as the police and child protection workers, it is also difficult to address risk and safety concerns when there are so many unknowns. Even when information is provided by the family about their pre-and post-migration journey, service providers can feel overwhelmed and they cannot respond to these elements within their mandated capacity and the expectations and work load they have to deal with. These feelings of being overwhelmed can lead many workers to make decisions to go back to their protocols as a safer way to cope. So there is no room for supporting the family to negotiate and navigate the broader service-providing system. My involvement with these kinds of complex cases showed me that there were big gaps between how the services work when supporting families with complex needs. The CIFSR book comes from real people like this, real situations, and actual workers. Once we have touched people, we are obligated to be creative and stretch beyond our limited experience. By engaging in this work, we grow to understand and see, and with that comes increased responsibility.

LYNDA: Can you say more about your primary goals in engaging in CIFSR-guided work?

MOHAMMED: I would describe the work I have been doing, including the CIFSR guide, as trying to bring potential "enemies" together to start a conversation rather than pointing fingers and fighting. When someone is passionate about supporting a victim, then the husband or the community is seen as the enemy. If they can work with me, I can help them see each other as human beings without compromising safety and accountability concerns. Child protection workers, fathers, and mothers can communicate as human beings when we slow down the process and engage with this person as a husband and father. I see "strengths-based" as meaning "human." I think it is important to see risk as dynamic. For example, I learned of a situation where there was great concern about parental neglect because the children of the family were running around their new neighbourhood without shoes on their feet and unsupervised. When this concern was raised with the mother, she expressed surprise – she saw her new neighbourhood as quite safe because there were no landmines, and she welcomed the freedom this brought to her children. She saw herself as far from neglectful as she had kept her children safe in an extremely dangerous situation before migration. Context, of course, is very important in understanding relative risk and safety.

LYNDA: I know that you've shared your ideas in Chapter 6 about how the CIFSR model compares with other culturally grounded practices, but I wonder if you could say a bit more about your experience of CIFSR in practice?

MOHAMMED: The key to CIFSR is the partnerships between "mainstream" service providers and cultural organizations like MRCSSI. I don't believe that it is enough to simply have diverse cultural and linguistic representation in the staff at a service-providing organization. What is different about the CIFSR model is that the cultural organization comes in at a partnership level, equal with other organizations, and this is key. This partnership respects the status of all of the key players, and ensures that all are part of the planning. CORT is not just a crisis response, but it brings together the key people who have responsibility in this situation. We want a response that is creative and honours what is valuable to this woman and this family; we want to hear her dilemma. She wants her family, but she needs also to be safe. We need to make sure the voices of the key people important to those who are at risk of violence are included in the solution in order to provide long-term support for those who are more vulnerable. The CIFSR model supports frontline workers in service-provider organizations – cultural capacity is important, but most important is that the manager supports worker flexibility and knows who else to listen to. This is where the cultural organization comes in and provides links to the community. Engaging the community as part of the solution is so important. For example, if men and women are religious, they see themselves as accountable to a superior power. The imam can be a valuable ally in such circumstances. We want, however, to not only come to him in crisis, but to build an ongoing relationship with him. And established organizations don't always see the marginalized community without support to do so. We have introduced the Shared Journeys Project in communities where the initial response has been that "we don't really have that population here," and I say "wait and see." Once the program is in place, the community becomes more visible.

LYNDA: How do you see working in this way as making a difference?

MOHAMMED: We have been able to do a lot of preventative work in the last few years. You don't see this type of work in the news. Many cases are dealt with in less intrusive ways, avoiding the complexity and confusion in other communities which become difficult to stop. This preventative work contributes to building personal relationships. In many situations, working with the Children's Aid Society in complex cases, I have heard senior staff of this organization tell me that they respond differently based on our consultation because they trust us. With this message comes big responsibility and big change – people begin to believe in themselves and others. Adding the cultural piece allows us to have a meaningful response.

LYNDA: How would you like to see us build on this?

MOHAMMED: I'm excited about this book because I see that it can provide a foundation for building a training curriculum. I also see the opportunity to encourage mandated services to stretch their current practices and protocols to meet and respond to the complex situation of refugees and newcomers.

LYNDA: I see what you mean Mohammed – I think the act of writing this all down in a coherent manner, and me asking you questions, and both of us noticing when it got a bit muddled, has been really helpful in clarifying how we talk about the processes of CIFSR-guided work. I think we got clearer on describing the continuum of response, and how this intersected with differential responses and what to be paying close attention to when it comes to risk and context for safety. What I appreciated most of all was being able to present case examples. I know that I then asked more questions (it's what we therapists do best) and we got to talk more (which I always appreciate). In furthering the conversation, I know that I extended my own understanding of some of the initially overlooked aspects in our descriptions of how the CORT came together or what the FAST highlighted. This level of detail, and careful consideration of the process, provides new ways to understand how the model works and maybe provides more information for others who might be thinking about how to adapt it to their context. Something that I know very clearly is that the cultural organization coming in at the partnership level – seen as equal to other service providers and as bringing key information about culture, ethnicity, and community to the table – is critical to CIFSR-guided work. To co-opt these ideas without that critical partnership and granting status to cultural knowledge and relationships within the community is to miss the point of the model. Even as a culturally informed or culturally sensitive professional, if I am not part of the socioethnic collectivist community and not a newcomer, or have not experienced pre-migration trauma or shared the life experience of transglobal migration between very different dominant cultural contexts, I can't fully appreciate or understand the complex experience of the persons/communities I am serving. The role of the cultural broker – to ensure ongoing relationships, to build cultural capital and awareness, to provide a context of understanding complexities, and to provide information and guidance along the way – is critical to the working of this model. That, and relationship building – maybe you could say some more about that Mohammed?

MOHAMMED: I hope that this book encourages established service providers to revise their understanding of diversity practices and outreach. It is difficult to share learning with other organizations when there is no history of relationship. For example, in our current context, settlement organizations are the gateway for all newcomers. These organizations are mainstream, government funded, and have established practice standards. There are, however, limits to putting a portion of the population into this one box. A contemporary child protection worker or settlement worker who speaks Arabic is quite different in his/her own life experience than a current Syrian refugee, for example. This professional, trained perhaps in a Canadian context, working in an organization that is established and regulated by the Canadian government, and guided by professional standards, is likely more limited in his/her gaze than more diverse voices present in the local community. If we shift the paradigm to see beyond providers and recipients of education, and instead focus on establishing partnerships, we will find ways to know this community and go where the people are. Find out how many are in these communities. Who can connect you to this community? Have an initial conversation with no agenda. Go with an intention of wanting to work together, but wanting to know others better in order to start that. Or set up a pilot project. Use community mapping over a longer term. Ask someone from your organization to be a link, to collaborate with a local cultural organization to start a conversation and a direction for mapping. You don't have to make these other organizations part of your interventions initially. But with increased conversations you may consider using the CIFSR model, starting with this main group, developing a memorandum of understanding for proceeding. Be flexible and don't rush. Plan for a year, identify the key groups you want to see involved, then plan a mechanism for coordinating mandated action and communities.

LYNDA: You know Mohammed, we've talked about this before, and the relationship building is one of the parts of the CIFSR model that is most exciting to me. I think that we can learn from collectivist communities about how to do a better job of meeting people where they are when we are offering support or helping them out of difficulties. A professional organization in our Canadian context isn't often encouraged to build bridges with more informal community supports in people's lives. Funding and timesheets rarely prioritize these activities. But these informal supports, particularly those that represent faith perspectives or cultural traditions or day-to-day life activities, probably have more status or authority in a person's life than an unknown professional would have, especially when there is a feeling of being at risk or unsafe. I think we can do a lot better job of training new professionals to see the potential resources in a community, to engage in the longer-term process of building relationships across sectors and communities, to see value in the time that is invested in these, and to consider how this intersects with organizational structure and social policy.

MOHAMMED: I think we've touched on some implications for policies and procedures at an organizational and broader community level. For example, I would like to see organizations pay explicit attention to considering both cultural difference and migration experience when interviewing refugees and immigrants.

LYNDA: I'd like to pause for a moment and underline that brief statement you just made. This sounds like a subtle difference, but I think it makes a world of difference. Particularly for professionals who are more personally removed from the migration experience by generations and life experience, it can seem like "back home" is "back home" and "moving" is "moving," but we've demonstrated over and over here in our case examples that migration experience is both widely varied, unique to each person/family, and critical to understanding someone's current context. Simply exploring cultural difference without explicit attention to migration experience is insufficient – let's write that really large.

MOHAMMED: The timing is actually very good right now for paying attention to the implications of our work for social policy. With the large number of refugee families, some coming to Canada, many to European countries and even more displaced within the Middle East, the system is more receptive to modifying established responses. I think this allows a consideration of drawing distinctions between potential and actual risk, and between situational and chronic risk, for example. This may be the time to begin to provide a differential response to refugee communities that is based on the unique aspects of their experience vis-à-vis other newcomer communities. Perhaps this also calls for specially trained and culturally connected workers who work specifically with refugee families. This is a good time to think about creative organizational practices for serving newcomers and refugee communities. Perhaps future settlement agencies will provide access to a broader range of services and supports for diverse families.

LYNDA: Mohammed, you and I have had lots of really interesting conversations over the years, and I have really appreciated those. In fact, I feel quite privileged to have been a partner in the dialogue that has spanned so much development and refinement of this model and these practices. And I've also really appreciated the opportunities I've had over the years to have conversations with Eugene, Yasmin, Nada, Sahar, Hassna, and Abir, and recognize how much I have learned from their perspectives in working with the families they have supported. We've both talked about our excitement in what the future dialogues will contain when we put these ideas out into the broader world.

MOHAMMED: Yes, I would really like to invite our readers to contribute to extending this conversation. There are ongoing questions about this work that warrant a fuller conversation. How do we not compromise supports for vulnerable persons while also acknowledging the others within the family system? How can we best develop differential responses to refugees who arrive from conflict zones? More recently in Canada, police services have been paying particular attention to how best to respond to individuals who have mental health and addictions concerns. I would like for us to similarly engage in discussions of migration as an important consideration as it intersects with police services and the criminal justice system, in particular in a family violence context. These can be quite uncomfortable topics of conversation for many victims' services professionals.

In fact MRCSSI and many other established service providers such as settlement agencies, mental health services, social services, child protection services, and victims' services, as well as women's services, have very recently come together in our city, London, Ontario, to come up with better strategies to respond to the current increased number of Syrian refugees coming here. The city, in collaboration with many community services including MRCSSI, has established different committees to coordinate community responses. We have been able to reach out to Syrian refugees staying in hotels, neighbourhoods, churches, and mosques. We have already initiated working groups with many agencies on particular cases that involve risk factors of family violence and implementing our FAST and CORT approaches. As a result of this success in the current situations, MRCSSI has become a lead agency to coordinate early intervention programs with respect to family violence, in particular for situations related to child abuse and neglect. We have had several meetings with the leaders of the local child protection agency, settlement organization, newcomer medical clinic, police family consultants and victims' services, and the school board. We have now a working group where all cases related to child protection are referred. In one of our meetings, the executive director of the London and Middlesex

Children's Aid Society, Regina Bell, said "we should learn how to slow down the process when we respond to reports of child abuse within refugee families." She added that

> child safety continues to be the priority. We need to intentionally understand pre-migration experiences of the family in order to ensure that timely, culturally and spiritually relevant assessments and interventions occur. We need to recognize and mobilize the strengths within the family, community, and partnerships in the co-creating of solutions.

It is very interesting for me to see that many organizations and leaders of established services who were not sure about the culturally integrative model of response are now coming to our organization to seek advice and expressing willingness to be part of this new venture. In the first four months since the first of the most recent groups of Syrian refugees have come to Canada, we have dealt with more than 15 serious local situations involving family violence and including woman abuse and child abuse. Only one of these cases escalated to a point that the woman and her children were at high risk and we have separated her and her children from her husband. The police and the court were involved but we still provided support and services for the children, the woman, and her husband separately. We are fortunate to be able to reach out to the rest of these families through our collaboration with the settlement organization, Cross Cultural Learner Centre, as early as possible. In this way, we can interrupt the escalation of violence and provide women and men with the support they need before conflicts escalate and result in tragedies. All of this shows that the CIFSR has been working well in our community. When the most recent Syrian refugees came to our community, we were ready to respond to their needs in a culturally meaningful way.

One of the exciting new programs that MRCSSI is leading now is called the Safe Integration Support (SIS) groups. During Phase 1, the SIS groups are focused on creating a place for mothers, fathers, and youth to share their stories and reflect upon their journeys. SIS groups are grounded within a strengths-based and culturally integrative approach, and create opportunities for interactive dialogue through a process facilitated in Arabic and a culturally meaningful manner. These groups create a place for active dialogue and reflection, and invite mothers, fathers, and families to share their values and strengths, as well as their hopes and concerns, with each other. SIS groups serve to create a place in which individuals and families have an opportunity to share what is important to them as they start their lives in Canada. The group sessions also serve as an important opportunity for individuals and families to identify needs and participate in the process of mapping ongoing support and programming priorities. Further, SIS groups function as a preventative and early-intervention strategy with respect to issues of family violence. These groups provide an opportunity for MRCSSI staff to learn about how refugees are experiencing the process of settlement and integration, how to identify stressors and situations of vulnerability and risk, as well as how to assess resiliencies, vulnerability, and risk. More importantly, the relationships developed within SIS groups between participants and MRCSSI staff create opportunities for further, more targeted, early-intervention supports and responses with specific individuals and families if deemed necessary based upon these early assessments.

LYNDA: Mohammed, I wonder if you could talk a bit more about risk factors and challenging the way we talk about and see these, particularly in relation to religion?

MOHAMMED: Culture and religion are often closely intertwined, perhaps particularly for collectivist families and including Muslims. Religious beliefs are held as a moral reference, and this has been used historically to justify violence in certain contexts. Overlapping cultural and religious principles are reflected in social norms that act as a set of beliefs guiding many families to determine what appropriate and inappropriate behaviour is. This is why it is important to know the importance of religious beliefs in the lives of the respective families we are assessing with regard to risk. This has to move beyond stereotypes. Using a religious lens allows us to better understand how people make sense of abuse or violent behaviour. At the same time, however, we should not conclude that, because you are a Muslim or a religious person, you are a controlling person in intimate partner relationships.

When we have a better sense of risk sources, then we can invite the right people to support safety and address risk. In doing so, our approach to engage religious or community leaders will be inviting and welcoming. This way we can expect more from religious authorities in terms of their obligation to protect those who seek guidance and help from them. We can, in my experience, push the envelope in working with religious leaders and hold them accountable for their views and messages about violence. It is important, in these endeavours, from the beginning to honour the status of a religious leader. From that position of respect, we can then engage in training and building awareness about warning signs, duty to report, and the consequences of violence. At MRCSSI, we have already started the conversation with the imams and some key leaders within the London Muslim community. We want to develop a protocol of understanding that ensures the imams will be trained to recognize warning signs of family violence and how they can be more helpful to women and children, as well as men who could be violent or abusive in their intimate relationships.

LYNDA: This is difficult work Mohammed, and these are also complex and challenging conversations to have. I do look forward to hearing what our readers have to say, and how the dialogues will unfold from here. I find myself wondering about how the CIFSR model might be adapted to other cultural contexts – for example, could these ideas serve as a guide for bridging formal and informal services in nonindigenous and indigenous communities; how might the CIFSR model need to be altered to best fit with non-Muslim and non-Arab communities; and will the model demonstrate adaptability over time as newcomer communities become more established? I imagine that our readers will have many thoughts about how the model does and doesn't fit with their current context or challenges. I especially think that the roles of relationship building across communities and of listening to each other and respecting the leaders and mentors within the local communities will be key in any extension of the CIFSR model. I also want to thank you for the opportunity to collaborate in capturing where the dialogue is for us at this moment in time, and state publicly that I look forward to our ongoing conversations.

MOHAMMED: Lynda, this is really a great opportunity for me also to collaborate with you in this book. I see this book as a very important milestone in our ongoing collaboration and conversations over the years. It has been great to see that both of us have grown in this process and actually I can also see it as a model of integrating both personal and professional aspects of the relationship that led to this very important work. What we have been doing is an example that people from different backgrounds can work together toward defined common goals that would lead to greater impact and positive change. I can see how our collaboration is related to overall work we have been doing for the last few years. Within each community there are those who are interested in engaging change. It is important to mobilize these people. It takes time – relationship building requires that as well as place. We work to try to find the light.

Appendix A
Four Aspects Screening Tool (FAST)

Universal Aspect

Demographics

(Insert/attach agency intake form)
Name: ....
Date of birth (yyyy / mm / dd): ....
Country of origin: ....
Citizen status:

- ☐ Government-assisted refugee
- ☐ Refugee claimant
- ☐ Permanent resident
- ☐ Canadian citizen

Date of arrival to Canada (yyyy / mm / dd): ....
Prior residences (where they came from):

- ☐ I come from an urban area in my country of origin: ....
- ☐ I have lived in another country (transit) before coming to Canada: ....

Family Structure

Partner/Spouse: ....
Marital status and relationship dynamic:

- • Marital status: ....
- • Describe your current marriage: ....
- • Were you or your spouse ever married before this marriage? ....

Children:

- Do you have children from this marriage? ....
- Do you have children from previous marriages? ....
- The children of previous marriage(s) live with: ....

In-laws living with family:

☐ My in-laws live with us in the same home

Extended family member(s)/friends staying with family:

☐ My extended family lives with us
☐ We have friends living with us on a frequent basis

Summary of Family Structure:

- ....
+ ....

Universal Nature of Conflict/Presenting Issue

(Attach agency protocol assessment)
Family safety concerns:

- I describe my relationship with my family as: ....
- Presenting issue: ....

Individual response to safety concerns/conflicts (discipline/action/attitudes towards):

- I am dealing with the current situation: ....
- I view this issue: ....

Summary of Presenting Issues/Nature of Conflict and Differing Responses to Presenting Issue:

- ....
+ ....

Health

Physical health conditions/symptoms:

☐ I have been suffering from health problems: ....

☐ I have been diagnosed by a doctor to have (name sickness): ....
☐ I experience pain which interferes with my daily life: ....

Emotional health issues/stressors:

☐ My anxieties and worries prevent me from sleeping well at night
• I worry about: ....
• I am scared by: ....

Mental health issues/stressors:

☐ Anything can irritate me in the time being
☐ I am sad/depressed most of the time
• I usually deal with my sad/depressed feelings by taking: ....

Summary of Health Status:

- ....
+ ....

Education

Level of schooling completed and tacit knowledge/apprenticeship:

• I have completed this much schooling: ....

Professional training in Canada:

☐ I have received education in Canada: ....
• Difference in educational qualifications/accreditation in Canada: ....
☐ My education has been recognized here in Canada
☐ My profession has not been recognized in Canada

Educational barriers:

☐ I have faced educational barriers here in Canada: ....

Summary of Education:

- ....
+ ....

Family Economics

Job status/current occupation:

- ☐ I am currently working in my original profession

Difference in job status from country of origin:

- ☐ My job status is different from my country of origin (for example, maybe now at entry level)
- ☐ I have financial hardships

Current situation:

- ☐ My partner works
- ☐ My partner's work poses a challenge to her/his role in the family
- ☐ My partner contributes to the household finances by sharing the expenses

Basic supports/stressors:

- ☐ I am able to support my family's basic needs

Income supports/stressors:

- ☐ My financial hardships impact negatively my relationship with my partner/spouse
- ☐ My financial hardships impact negatively my relationship with my children

Summary of Financial Situation:

- ....
+ ....

Family Support (Providing or Receiving)

Family support (financial):

- ☐ I receive financial support from my extended family
- ☐ I support financially a family member(s) back home
- ☐ I am obligated to support financially the family member(s) to whom I am sending money

Summary of Financial Support/Stressors:

- ....
+ ....

Recommended Key CORT Partner(s): ....
Examples of Recommended Key CORT Partner(s):

- Family doctor
- Employment counselor
- Child protection worker
- Ontario Works worker
- Housing stability worker
- Teacher

Migration Aspect

Migration Experience

Pre-migratory experience: ....
Experiences of life in country of origin and/or place of prior residence:
....
Armed conflict areas:

- ☐ I lived in my country of origin in an armed conflict zone
- ☐ I left my area of residence to another area to secure my family safety within my country
- ☐ My family and I were forced to leave my country to another country for safety reasons

Summary of Migration Experience:

- ....
+ ....

Witnessing Experiences of War and Conflict

Nature of conflicts: ....
Armed conflicts (tribal/inter-group/ethno-racial/religious):

- ☐ I have been subjected to acts of violence in my home country

- ☐ I have witnessed a family member being subjected to acts of violence in my home country
- ☐ My family and I have experienced loss of family members/friends/ neighbours

Effects of witnessing conflict:

- ☐ I was able to handle my daily living well during the armed conflict
- ☐ I was able to protect my family during conflict times
- ☐ I have faced imminent dangers in fleeing from one area to another in my country

Summary of Witnessed Conflicts:

- ....

+ ....

Post Migration

Integration and adjusting: ....

Journey to Canada: ....

Socioeconomic status of the family: ....

Adjustment to Canadian context:

- ☐ Upon arrival to Canada, my family and I have an orientation that helped us navigate the Canadian system (services)
- ☐ I have faced many challenges in adjusting to the Canadian culture

Shift in socioeconomic status:

- ☐ My socioeconomic status has declined drastically in Canada
- ☐ I face socioeconomic hardship due to my inability to work in my profession

Identified barriers to adjustment process:

- ☐ I am facing challenges in my new environment

Community involvement and support (Canadian context):

- ☐ I spend my free time with my family
- ☐ My family and I are engaged in the Canadian celebrations

☐ I participate in volunteer work in community (organization/school/ neighbourhood)

Summary of Integration Challenges:

- ....
+ ....

Recommended Key CORT Partner(s): ....
Examples of Recommended Key CORT Partner(s):

- Counsellor/psychologist
- Social worker
- Settlement worker
- Lawyer

Ethno-cultural Aspect

Cultural Dynamics

Tribe/Culture: ....
Culture/identity of family:

- My cultural background is: ....
- Tell me about your cultural background: ....
- I identify myself as (ethnicity): ....

Summary of Cultural Dynamics:

- ....
+ ....

Family Dynamics

Gender role(s) in family:

☐ I consider myself as the main head of the family
☐ I am in charge of my family's well-being

Role changes in the family after coming to Canada:

☐ My responsibilities toward my family have changed

- ☐ My partner has a more active role as the head of the family than me
- ☐ My role as the breadwinner has changed within my family

Relationship dynamics:

- ☐ I have difficulties communicating with my family members
- ☐ I am the one who works out conflicts within my household

Parent-child dynamics (when parent is being interviewed):

- ☐ My relationship with my children is conflictual
- ☐ I have high expectations of school achievement for my children
- ☐ I have high expectations of my children to live according to my values and beliefs

Child-parent dynamics (if youth/child is being interviewed):

- ☐ My relationship with my parents is conflictual
- ☐ My parents' expectations of me are impossible
- ☐ My parents take decisions on my behalf

Role of extended family in daily life and decision making:

- ☐ My relationships with other members of my extended family are good
- ☐ My extended family interferes with my family decisions

Family supports (siblings/parents/extended family members):

- ☐ I reach out to when I have problems with my family (specify who and what relationship): ....
- ☐ My family member who is my support lives close to my home
- ☐ My family member who is my support offers me psychological and emotional support

Summary of Family Dynamics:

- ....
+ ....

Sense of Belonging/Support and Safety:

Level of connection/belonging to ethno-cultural community:

☐ I am connected to my ethnic community here in Canada

Identified sources of support:

☐ I regard the ethnic leader of my community as an important support to me
☐ My ethnic leader helps me through advice and being there for me
☐ I accept and access any supports offered from my network of friends or social group

Summary of Sources of Support:

- ....
+ ....

Recommended Key CORT Partner(s): ....
Examples of Recommended Key CORT Partner(s):

• Community leader
• Settlement worker
• Extended family member

Religious and Faith Aspect

Religious/Faith Views

Religious affiliation:

☐ I am a religious person
☐ I fully abide by the religious rituals
☐ I belong to the same religion/faith as my whole family

Role/impact of religion/faith in daily life:

☐ Religion guides my life in every aspect
☐ My religion has impacted my marriage positively
☐ My religion rules my relationship with my family

Summary of the Impact of Religion/Faith:

- ....
+ ....

Role/Impact of Religion/Faith in Family

- ☐ My extended family is religious
- ☐ Religion/faith guides my extended family daily living

Summary of Differences in Role/Impact of Religion in Family:

- ....
+ ....

Support/Belonging to Religious Community

- ☐ I am supported by my religious community
- ☐ I have a sense of belonging to my religious community
- ☐ I am engaged in my religious community

Summary of Religious Affiliation and Influences:

- ....
+ ....

Recommended Key CORT Partner(s): ....

Examples of Recommended Key CORT Partner(s):

- Imam
- Religious leader
- Friends within religious community
- Family members

Appendix B
Glossary of Acronyms and Organizations

CAS	Children's Aid Society
CASLM	Children's Aid Society of London and Middlesex, London, Ontario, Canada – child protection agency
CIFSR	Culturally Integrative Family Safety Response model
CORT	Coordinated Organizational Response Teams
FAST	The Four Aspects Screening Tool utilized for assessment in collectivist immigrant and newcomer communities
IPV	Intimate partner violence
MFSP	Muslim Family Safety Project – precursor organization to MRCSSI, London, Ontario, Canada – established in 2003
MOSAIC	Multilingual Orientation Service Association for Immigrant Communities, British Columbia, Canada
MRCSSI	Muslim Resource Centre for Social Support and Integration, London, Ontario, Canada – established in 2009
PAR	Partner Assault Response programs for men
PCHS	Punjabi Community Health Services, Peel Region, Ontario, Canada
PTSD	Post-traumatic stress disorder
Reclaim Honour Project	MRCSSI community-based violence prevention project. Funded by Status of Women Canada, 2013
Shared Journeys Project	MRCSSI project to transfer model of collaboration between child protection and cultural organization from London, Ontario to other Ontario communities. Funded by the Ontario Trillium Foundation, an agency of the Government of Ontario, 2012–2014
SIP	Safe Integration Project – MRCSSI and London Cross Cultural Learner Centre joint program to support newcomer families exposed to pre-migration trauma (migration from conflict zones). Funded by Ontario Trillium Foundation and Ontario Ministry of the Attorney General, 2011–2014

Bibliography

Baobaid, M. (2008). Community service responses towards men's violence against women and children in the context of pre-migration experiences. Unpublished manuscript.

Bowles, R. (2001). Social work with refugee survivors of torture and trauma. In M. Alston & J. McKinnon (eds), *Social work: Fields of practice* (249–267). New York: Oxford University Press.

Brown, L. (2009). Cultural competence: A new way of thinking about integration in therapy. *Journal of Psychotherapy Integration*, 19(4), 340–353. doi: 10.1037/a0017967

Dutton, M. A., Orloff, L. E., & Hass, G. A. (2000). Characteristics of help-seeking behaviours, resources and service needs of battered immigrant Latinas: Legal and policy implications. *Georgetown Journal on Poverty Law & Policy*, 7(2), 245–305.

Dwairy, M. (2002). Foundations of psychosocial dynamic personality theory of collective people. *Clinical Psychology Review*, 22(3), 343–360. doi: 10.1016/S0272–7358(01)00100–00103

Eisenman, D., Gelberg, H. U., & Shapiro, M. F. (2003). Mental health and health-related quality of life among adult Latino primary care patients living in the United States with previous exposure to political violence. *Journal of the American Medical Association*, 290(6), 627–634. doi: 10.1001/jama.290.5.627

Gilligan, C. (1982). *In a different voice: Psychological theory and women's development.* Cambridge, MA: Harvard University Press.

Goodman, L. & Epstein, D. (2005). Refocusing on women: A new direction for policy and research on intimate partner violence. *Journal of Interpersonal Violence*, 20(4), 479–487. doi: 10.1177/0886260504267838

Gupta, J., Acevedo-Garcia, D., Hemenway, D., Decker, M., Raj, A., & Silverman, J. (2009). Premigration exposure to political violence and perpetration of intimate partner violence among immigrant men in Boston. *American Journal of Public Health*, 99(3), 462–469. doi: 10.2105/AJPH,2007.120634

Haj-Yahia, M. & Sadan, E. (2008). Issues in intervention with battered women in collectivist societies. *Journal of Marital and Family Therapy*, 34(1), 1–13. doi: 10.1111/j.1752–0606.2008.00049.x

Hancock, T. U., Ames, N., & Behnke, A. O. (2014). Protecting rural church-going immigrant women from family violence. *Journal of Family Violence*, 29(3), 323–332. doi: 10.1007/s10896–10014–9581-x

Jiwani, Y. (2005). Walking a tightrope: The many faces of violence in the lives of racialized immigrant girls and young women. *Violence Against Women*, 11(7), 846–875. doi: 10.1177/1077801205276273

Jordan, J., Kaplan, A., Miller, J., Stiver, I., & Surrey, J. (eds). (1991). *Women's growth in connection: Writings from the Stone Centre*. New York: The Guilford Press.

Kanagartnam, P., Mason, R., Hyman, I., Manuel, L., Berman, H., & Toner, B. (2012). Burden of womanhood: Tamil women's perceptions of coping with intimate partner violence. *Journal of Family Violence*, 27(7), 647–658. doi: 10.1007/s10896–10012–9461–9461

Korteweg, A. & Selby, A. (2012). *Debating Sharia: Islam, gender politics, and family law arbitration*. Toronto: University of Toronto Press.

Krug, E., Dahlberg, L., Mercy, J., Zwi, A., & Lozano, R. (eds). (2002). *World report on violence and health*. Geneva: World Health Organization.

Madsen, W. (2014). Taking it to the streets: Family therapy and family-centered services. *Family Process*, 53(3), 380–400. doi: 10.1111/famp.12089

Markus, H. & Kitayama, S. (1994). A collective fear of the collective: Implications for selves and theories of selves. *Personality and Social Psychology Bulletin*, 20(5), 568–579. doi: 10.1177/0146167294205013

Raj, A. & Silverman, J. G. (2002). Intimate partner violence against South Asian women in greater Boston. *Journal of the American Medical Women's Association*, 57(2), 111–114.

Rousseau, C. & Drapeau, A. (2004). Premigration exposure to political violence among independent immigrants and its association with emotional distress. *Journal of Nervous & Mental Disease*, 192(12), 852–856. doi: 10.1097/01.nmd.0000146740.66351.23

Sokoloff, N. (2008). Expanding the intersectional paradigm to better understand domestic violence in immigrant communities. *Critical Criminology*, 16, 229–255. doi: 10.1007/s10612–10008–9059–9053

Struthers, M. (2013). Fair exchange: Public funding for social impact through the non-profit sector. Metcalf Foundation, June, p. 15. URL: http://metcalffoundation.com/wp-content/uploads/2013/06/FairExchange.pdf

Tervalon, M. & Murray-Garcia, J. (1998). Cultural humility versus cultural competence: A critical distinction in defining physician training outcomes in multicultural education. *Journal of Health Care for the Poor and Underserved*, 9(2), 117–125.

Yoishioka, M. & Choi, D. (2005). Culture and interpersonal violence research: Paradigm shift to create a full continuum of domestic violence services. *Journal of Interpersonal Violence*, 20(4), 513–519. doi: 10.1177/0886260504267758

Index

Page numbers in italics refer to figures.